other duties

as assigned

ASCD cares about Planet Earth.
This book has been printed on environmentally friendly paper.

other
duties
as assigned

JAN BURGESS
with donna bates

ASCD Alexandria, Virginia USA

1703 N. Beauregard St. • Alexandria, VA 22311-1714 USA
Phone: 800-933-2723 or 703-578-9600 • Fax: 703-575-5400
Web site: www.ascd.org • E-mail: member@ascd.org
Author guidelines: www.ascd.org/write

Gene R. Carter, *Executive Director;* Nancy Modrak, *Publisher;* Scott Willis, *Director, Book Acquisitions & Development;* Genny Ostertag, *Acquisitions Editor;* Julie Houtz, *Director, Book Editing & Production;* Katie Martin, *Editor;* Greer Wymond, *Senior Graphic Designer;* Mike Kalyan, *Production Manager;* Valerie Younkin, *Desktop Publishing Specialist;* Kyle Steichen, *Production Specialist*

All Web links in this book are correct as of the publication date below but may have become inactive or otherwise modified since that time. If you notice a deactivated or changed link, please e-mail books@ascd.org with the words "Link Update" in the subject line. In your message, please specify the Web link, the book title, and the page number on which the link appears.

PAPERBACK ISBN: 978-1-4166-0886-8   ASCD product #109075   n12/09

Also available as an e-book (see Books in Print for the ISBNs).

Quantity discounts for the paperback edition only: 10–49 copies, 10%; 50+ copies, 15%; for 1,000 or more copies, call 800-933-2723, ext. 5634, or 703-575-5634. For desk copies: member@ascd.org.

Library of Congress Cataloging-in-Publication Data
Burgess, Jan, 1949-
  Other duties as assigned : tips, tools, and techniques for expert teacher leadership / Jan Burgess ; with Donna Bates.
    p. cm.
  Includes bibliographical references and index.
  ISBN 978-1-4166-0886-8 (pbk. : alk. paper) 1. Teacher participation in administration. 2. Educational leadership. I. Bates, Donna. II. Title.
  LB2806.45.B87 2009
  371.1'06–dc22
                                                                          2009031205

20 19 18 17 16 15 14 13 12 11 10 09   1 2 3 4 5 6 7 8 9 10 11 12

**Build structures
and systems,
but leave the
door open
to serendipity.**

–Garnetta Wilker

other duties
as assigned

Tips, Tools, and Techniques for Expert Teacher Leadership

acknowledgments

This book is a compilation of ideas and practices garnered from many sources. Jan is indebted to her collaborator, Donna Bates, a teacher leader with whom she shares a passion for teaching and learning—particularly at the middle levels—with an appreciation of the gifts, the talents, and the heart that so many bring to our profession.

Jan is forever grateful for the guidance, patience, analysis, and conceptual suggestion provided by Pete Lorain. He stopped whatever he was doing whenever she called on him and was a personal cheerleader from the inception of this manuscript through all the rewrites, late nights, and early morning walks.

The following school leaders, administrators, and teachers shared willingly what has worked for them in their schools and, conversely, what has not: Debbi Nagelmann, Linda Mihata, Pat Sharp and Nadine Lutz, Jared Condon, Nancy Poliseno and Jane Lierman, Garnetta Wilker, Lou Welsch, Kim Ball, Darrel Galera, Peter Langley, Margaret Calvert, Yelena Kniep, K. D. Parmein, and Aletia Cochran. To all of them, and to all other talented teacher leaders we have worked with over the years, our thanks.

introduction

None of us is as smart as all of us.

—Ken Blanchard

Much like a mosaic, in which many small, individual pieces combine to form a complete picture, schools are made up of individuals bound together for a singular purpose. When the people in the school share a common purpose and a clear focus, a dynamic picture emerges: one in which all students and staff are learning, engaged, and enthusiastic.

In any mosaic, the frame provides structure. The tiles give texture and color. Glue holds the many pieces together. In the complex and multifaceted mosaic that is a school, the framework is provided by the principal, who works to align the school's vision with district goals, state mandates, federal initiatives, and other external influences. The characteristics of and relationships among teachers, students, parents, and staff add the color and the tones to the school mosaic. When aligned for a common purpose, the connections between these individuals coalesce to form the whole: one that's more than the sum of its parts.

In the parts-to-a-whole equation, there is widespread agreement in professional literature about what effective principals do; there is similar agreement about what master teachers do. And while there is general agreement that teacher leaders play a critical role in the mosaic of effective schools, what *really* matters in teacher leadership—the real hows, whats, and whys of teachers leading teachers—can sometimes be lost amid the role's myriad duties, responsibilities, and pressures ... or left unaddressed due to a lack of leadership training.

The Structure of This Book

Other Duties as Assigned is a resource guide for teacher leaders that identifies the skills and processes necessary to lead a group of peers so that they function well together and become a team. To be effective in this role, teacher leaders need training and ongoing support. Principals and building administrators have a critical role to play in nurturing teacher leaders through technical assistance, capacity building, and troubleshooting. Their consistent articulation of a common vision is needed to sustain any effort to effect change through a team structure.

The dual threads of strengthening relationships and a collective focus on teaching and learning (for the adults in the school as well as for students) form the core of this book. Its chapters follow a standard format. Each begins with key ideas and brief research citations from the experts that set the context for that chapter. The text moves from research to practical application with prompts for you, the reader, to reflect on your own school and your own leadership practices. You'll find sample teacher leadership dilemmas, real-life questions and answers to common leadership challenges, and tools and resources that are practical, easily accessible, and support the ideas and themes of each chapter.

Let's take a closer look at each of these components.

Questions to Consider

Found in sidebars, these sets of questions reflect the general themes and concepts from the chapter narrative. They are meant to be interactive and thought provoking—to prompt you to reflect on your skills, your team of peers, your understanding of the leadership situation in which you find yourself, your goals, and your ideas about possible solutions and new directions. For example, consider the questions in the sidebar at right, and take a few moments to record the thoughts that come to you.

QUESTIONS
to Consider

···→ What does the principal need to have in place for the school to be successful?

···→ What roles can and should teacher leaders play?

···→ What types of support and resources are there for teacher leaders in your school?

···→ What would you need to know before you'd consider leading a group of your peers?

Leadership Dilemmas

Throughout the book, we will follow three teacher leaders: composites of the many teacher leaders Jan has worked alongside during her 30 years in public education. Ruben, Karen, and Elise find themselves facing dilemmas that are representative of the various teacher leader concerns, issues, and situations that occur in any school where teachers are organized into teams. Here is a thumbnail sketch of each of the three teacher leaders:

• Ruben is a middle-level science teacher and is new to the teacher leader position. He is charged with bringing together teachers from two small schools and integrating them into a single, grade-level team at a larger school.

• Karen works on a 5th and 6th grade team in an elementary school. After being a team member for six years, she's just been appointed as the team's new teacher leader.

• Elise is a veteran educator, with many years of teaching and leadership experience at both the junior high and high school levels. She is a department chair and has led various districtwide curriculum groups.

The dilemmas Ruben, Karen, and Elise face over the course of their year touch on the dynamics of the teacher leader role. With each scenario, you'll be prompted to reflect on the issues presented, consider the constraints and responsibilities the teacher leader faces, and formulate your own response. You'll find *keys* to guide your thinking—important points related to the two critical aspects of teacher leadership: relationships and a focus on teaching and learning. Each of these sections concludes with *our response*, which is one suggested way—but by no means the only way—that the teacher leader might address the dilemma.

Here's an example to start you out:

RUBEN'S DILEMMA

As a new teacher leader with five years teaching experience in middle-level math, Ruben was concerned his teammates would see his new role as quasi-administrative: less about teaching and kids and more about managing, directing, and overseeing their work. His team members joked about his "going over to the dark side." Ruben is someone who thinks of himself as a teacher first. He's not sure what he'll be expected do as a "team leader," or how he'll manage his as-yet-unknown responsibilities while still keeping teaching as his main focus. What will he need to give up? How should he start? How can he define his leadership role as continuing to be "one of us" rather than "us versus them"?

 CONSIDER THESE KEY IDEAS AS YOU THINK ABOUT RUBEN'S DILEMMA:

Relationships

• Teacher leaders must set realistic expectations for their leadership responsibilities.

• It takes time to move forward—and a steadfast focus on goals.

• Teacher leaders need to share their vision with their team and ask for commitment and support.

- Teacher leaders must communicate, listen carefully, and take the time to meet and talk about change.
- Teacher leaders ought to read everything they can get their hands on about leading a team and how to effect cultural change within a school.

Teaching and Learning

- The teacher leader's goal should be to focus team members on their number one priority: collective learning to improve classroom practice and student learning.
- Engaging a team in conversation about the professional learning goals members would like to pursue individually is a good catalyst for setting collective professional learning goals.

OUR RESPONSE TO RUBEN:
ESTABLISH RELATIONSHIPS TO MOVE THE TEAM FORWARD

It will be important for Ruben to think about what his personal goals and leadership goals are. He will want to share these with his principal and with his teacher teammates. Doing so will underscore his commitment to his students, as an advocate for teaching and learning, and to his school, as a voice for what happens there. With these understandings of his role in place, Ruben must continue to be organized, continue to strengthen relationships among teammates, and continue to develop a relationship with the principal and the school's other teacher leaders. He can model his style of leadership through what he says, the ways in which he champions the school's vision, and how he engages others in conversations about students and about teaching and learning.

We would also encourage Ruben to join several professional organizations and to read and share articles and other materials that address how to improve teaching and learning.

Tools and Resources

At various points in a chapter, you'll see prompts to applicable tools—forms and templates that will support your efforts to undertake the chapter's recommended practices. Blank copies of these tools are collected in an appendix, which we're calling "A Teacher Leader's Toolkit" (p. 135). Interactive versions of these tools are available for download in a password-protected PDF format from the ASCD Web site (www.ascd.org), and instructions for accessing these forms can be found on page 136.

Each chapter includes a set of annotated resources that support the chapter's theme. These include highly recommended articles and books (with directions to sections that are particularly relevant) and links to sample online tools and other aids for practical application

Expert Advice on Teacher Leadership

Donna Bates was both a team and curriculum teacher leader at Lake Oswego Junior High School in Lake Oswego, Oregon. At the end of each chapter, she provides practical advice to real-life questions she has received about teacher leadership (see the example on the facing page). Donna has extensive experience as an academic team leader, a department chair, and a new teacher leader mentor. She was a member of an 8th grade team recognized by the National Middle School Association with a 2003 Teams Who Make a Difference Award for Academic Excellence. Donna and Jan hope that in these "Dear Donna" sections, you will see your own questions asked and answered.

Getting the Most from This Book

This book is written for educators who are thinking about becoming teacher leaders, teacher leaders who are new to the role, and veteran teacher leaders interested in staying current and challenging themselves to grow professionally.

DEAR DONNA

 CHANGES IN THE WIND

DEAR DONNA,

Things are changing in our school! I have been the English department head at our high school for nearly 15 years, and my primary responsibilities have been to oversee the department's budget, order materials, disseminate information to the department personnel, and meet with department staff to review new textbooks. Once or twice a year we meet as a department to talk about our curriculum. Now, we have reorganized ourselves into cross-curricular teaching teams, and we meet together on a very regular basis. I do support this change, but I am at a loss as to how to conduct these meetings and what to do in them. Can you help me?

SHANNON IN ANCHORAGE

Dear Shannon,

It sounds like your school has moved to a professional learning community (PLC) model, which is what many schools are doing in an effort to tap the collective expertise of their teaching staff for the purpose of raising student achievement. Yes, in this format, your role as a teacher leader will change significantly. You now are in the business of building relationships and helping your department staff come together as a cohesive body of experts who discuss, share, design, and build programs that can be used to engage students at all levels of academic abilities. Resources abound on how to develop relationships and how to use those relationships to improve student achievement. Search the professional magazines, look for newly published books that outline strategies and procedures for doing this, and tap into the resources your local college or university may have available.

Donna

• For those of you considering a role in school leadership, *Other Duties as Assigned* will support the work you do with your school and with your team of colleagues. If this is your situation, you will get a sneak preview of what to expect. You might start at the beginning and read through the entire book, paying particular attention to the leadership tools and Questions to Consider in Chapters 1 and 2.

• If you are new to teacher leadership, jumping ahead to Chapter 3's look at team building might be worth your while. There, you will find information and the processes and sample tools all teams can use to stay organized and focused.

• A current teacher leader whose team needs a boost will be interested in Chapter 4's focus on strengthening relationships and its many ideas for celebrating success.

• And those of you who have the good fortune to work with a strong team of professionals and are ready to really push yourselves further in working on teaching and learning strategies, Chapter 5 is definitely for you, as are the tools in the Appendix.

Regardless of whether you read this book cover to cover or skip around to meet your particular needs, in these pages you'll find a plethora of ideas, tools, and techniques. Use the book to support your professional growth, and note skill areas that you would like to strengthen. Thumb through sections that pertain to your situation, earmark activities and resources you might use, and take the time to consider the questions for self-reflection. Jot down ideas, find conversation starters, and run off or download tools that will support your work and add these to your professional library. Read this book to reaffirm your faith in yourself as a leader and in your colleagues as teammates. And expect success!

1

shared leadership

In mid-August, the much anticipated "Welcome Back, Teachers" letter arrived from the new principal at Oregon's Lake Oswego Junior High School. This year's letter was different. It read like a teacher's to-do list:

> Dear Faculty and Staff,
>
> Welcome back! For our upcoming inservice day together, please
>
> - Bring two colored markers.
> - Bring three note cards, each one with an idea you have always wanted to investigate or try in your classroom.
> - Wear tennis shoes.
> - Bring a bottle of water. (We're going to be working hard!)
> - Leave your cell phone, doubts, I can'ts, and it won't works at home.
>
> See you at 8 a.m. on August 31 in the school cafeteria. Breakfast and lunch will be provided.
>
> Can't wait for us to get started,
>
> Your principal

This was definitely not business as usual!

A Culture of Interdependence

Consider rafting a river with a group of friends. There is a guide, there are charts and maps of the river, and there is a sense of adventure as the group descends into the water. There are challenges ahead—perhaps boulders under the water that could sink the raft. Whitewater rapids and currents of varying strength are downstream. The guide instructs the group to listen to his commands, asks that each person be alert to potential hazards, and trains the group to work together. Throughout the journey, the group's trust in their leader grows, as does their sense of exhilaration in doing something successful together.

Shared leadership in schools is a similar journey. Through collaboration, collegiality, community, cooperation, and communication, interdependence emerges and is nourished. *Interdependence* is quality of connection built on trust and respect. For schools, the vehicle for building interdependence is not a raft but groups of teachers organized into teams—grade-level groups, departments, and small professional learning communities, each headed by a leader who facilitates the group's work and guides it toward a common end. As a faculty develops a shared, organization-wide understanding of who they are and what they are about, they are increasingly able to engage in ongoing, meaningful conversation that, if wisely and carefully conducted, becomes action on behalf of students and marks progress toward identified goals.

Historically, schools have operated on a hierarchical model. There is a leader at the top, who is charged with overseeing groups of teachers, who are charged with overseeing groups of students. Although teachers and others on staff work side by side, eat together, laugh, and share stories together, for most of the day they work alone, in their own individual classrooms with the doors closed. The faculty might meet monthly to hear updates about upcoming events, budget issues, schoolwide behavioral concerns, and district messages. Faculty meetings seldom involve robust discussions on issues or tackle curricular or instructional undertakings. When decisions are made, everyone knows it's the principal who says what's what. It's the principal who manages the operation.

Over the past several decades, a new model of interdependence has emerged. Margaret Wheatley (2000) describes this approach as one in which "people organize together to accomplish more, not less" (p. 340). She goes on to note, "Behind every organizing impulse is the realization that by joining with others we can accomplish something important we could not accomplish alone."

Schools, as living systems, have a great capacity to organize and to bring energy and passion to the work they undertake. When the system works as an integrated whole, with everyone in the organization connected around a central purpose, a synergy happens that can propel a school forward. We see this happen, for example, when faculty members commit to fully implementing new, cross-grade instructional strategies for reading, and then reading scores go up. We see it when a school faculty faithfully conducts data reviews and provides an array of instructional supports designed to help students meet grade-level reading and math standards, and then increasing numbers of students meet these standards and go on to graduate.

The Challenge of Leadership

Leadership in learning institutions means everyone understands and embraces the school's vision for student success, and everyone on staff participates in the journey toward that end. As Charlotte Roberts writes in *The Fifth Discipline Fieldbook*, "An interdependent vision can be realized only through collaborative action, so relationships at work become central" (Senge, Kleiner, Roberts, Ross, & Smith, 1994, p. 231). To re-energize, redefine, or re-establish the school's direction so that it provides opportunities for all students to succeed, there must be a collective responsibility for strengthening relationships and for improving academic achievement. This is the challenge administrators and teacher leaders share.

Fortunately, there are strong models for us to follow. Numerous major longitudinal research studies of effective schools attribute gains in student achievement to the work of small learning communities, team structures, and collaborative decision making (Jackson, Davis, Aheel, & Bordonaro, 2000; Lipsitz & Felner, 1997; Marzano, 2003; National Association of Secondary School Principals, 2000; National Middle School Association, 2003, 2005). Similarly, in *The Fifth Discipline* (1990) Peter Senge references teams, decision making, and a task orientation as crucial for any learning organization. Robert J. Marzano (2003) provides additional insight when he identifies three components that are necessary for establishing an interdependent work environment: broadening the range of participants in conversation, sharing power, and enhancing interpersonal relationships. Correspondingly, literature on high school reform points to "twin pillars ... (1) instructional improvement and (2) structural changes that personalize learning" (Quint, 2008, p. 68).

However, structural changes do not automatically result in substantive conversations or strengthened relationships among the adults who populate the school. Fostering a culture of interdependence relies on more than the structural apparatus usually in place in schools, which includes the building's schedules, how space is used, which rooms are allocated to which programs, and how adults spend their time. For example, team teaching can be an effective structure, but teaching side by side should not presume the two teachers will have conversations about students' challenges with curricular concepts or about the instructional strategies in use. The building's schedule might allow a group of teachers to share a common planning time but that, too, does not guarantee the teachers will meet together to assess student work or solve problems related to curriculum alignment.

The truth is, the critical work of schools is done through relationships among people. These relationships must be nurtured and attended to so that conversations move beyond collegiality to collaboration and a commitment to improving one's practice. In fact, recent research reviews done by the National Staff Development Council (2008) identified working in teams as the model for strengthening teaching practices. Also important, according to Jacqueline Ancess, coordinator of the National Center for Restructuring Education, Schools and Teaching, is that teacher relationships be "caring [and] characterized by interdependency, trust, respect and a sense of collective responsibility for students and school outcomes" (2008, p. 50). As William D. Greenfield (2005) writes, "The challenge for a school leader is to spark and sustain such a dialogue and to work with and through teachers to develop a shared commitment to implementing the desired practices effectively" (p. 249).

Moving toward this vision of strong relationships and a focus on student success begins by renewing an understanding of the purpose of the collective work in a school. Like the river rafters setting out on their journey, a faculty needs to know where they are all going and what each individual must do to help the school reach that destination.

To successfully navigate a river, ongoing conversation is a must. In school environments, those who lead must be willing to reexamine existing structures and processes and consider how else the school might organize itself to achieve the desired ends. New structures to consider are those that strengthen collegial relationship and provide a forum for many parties to share their voices and contribute to the conversation about how to support learning. These structures go by many names: professional learning communities (PLCs), Critical Friends Groups, interdisciplinary teams, and departments.

QUESTIONS
to Consider

→ What is your vision for your school?

→ What current leadership model exists in your school?

→ How are decisions made in your school?

The Various "Looks" of Interdependence

Interdependence does look different depending on the school, the environment, and other variables. Let's consider a couple of examples.

At Fir Grove Elementary School in Beaverton, Oregon, a Title I school of about 500 students, all teachers are members of a grade-level team. In 2007, the principal assessed relationships in the grade-level teams, agreed with the teams' purpose, and challenged staff to focus more specifically on using their team time to become a professional learning community. Now, each week, one of the grade-level teams meets for the entire day as a PLC to discuss best practices, share effective lessons, and talk about ways to meet student needs. Making time for this embedded staff development has energized the Fir Grove faculty. They have been able to make their vision of ongoing teacher-led professional development a reality by leveraging a very traditional structure (grade-level teams) that was already in place.

Then there is Lake Oswego Junior High School, where teachers are organized into four core academic teams for instruction and also divided into curriculum departments. Both groups—teams and departments—meet regularly, often during weekly early-release time, to engage in professional growth activities and build relationships between and among colleagues. These complementary structures provide two avenues for adults to get to know one another better, to work together, to support each other, and to share student-related concerns and successes. Additionally, having two organizational structures increases the number of teacher leaders who have a significant voice in the workings of the school.

As Gordon Donaldson (2006) puts it, "Leadership is about how I can help cultivate relationships among talented and well-intentioned educators and parents so that we all can assure that every child learns" (p. 3). Changing the culture from one in which the principal is the only leader to one in which there is collective ownership of the work of schools and many voices are heard is a powerful practice and, in some schools, requires a shift in perspective. With this model, we're no longer talking about a single raft guided by a single expert but an arrangement in which the river guide must depend on multiple leaders in multiple rafts to be alert to the challenges and obstacles of the journey and to move together in some systematic fashion for the success of the outing.

Sharing Leadership

A shared leadership model of governance means principals seek out others in their school to build partnerships, tap others' strengths, and jointly move the vision forward. Principals who believe and act in ways that are invitational and support a common purpose understand that strong relationships with their faculty, developed through both formal and informal interactions, is fundamental to motivating everyone to move in the same direction. Think of how multiple boats on a rafting trip reach their final destination. Some rafts will run the rapids; others will portage around the rapids to reach calmer waters. Each raft takes the route that's best suited to the skills of the group onboard. What really matters is that all rafts travel to and reach the same destination; for schools, that destination is improved student learning.

Remember the "Welcome Back, Teachers" letter at Lake Oswego Junior High? The new principal who wrote it was making the point that business as usual was changing. On that late August morning, the 46-member faculty met and moved directly into an all-school team-building activity. Each person relied on the next to complete the activity. Debriefing afterward over a picnic lunch, the faculty identified the strength of the activity as the opportunity to work together and talk with one another. The general mood was that they were all in it together, sink or swim, and they were glad to have partners to help them succeed. After lunch, the entire faculty engaged in a lengthy discussion about the focus for the upcoming year and brainstormed ways to keep positive team spirit alive. Everyone was invited to participate in the creation of the school's action plan and focus for the year. The day ended with department teams aligning their goals to the school's common emphasis. In this simple way, one school moved toward a new model of shared leadership.

RUBEN'S DILEMMA

Ruben is a 7th grade science teacher in a very crowded K–8 school. The district's second K–8 school has seen its enrollment drop dramatically and has classrooms to spare. In response, the school board announced a change to the current configuration: The two schools will have one year to examine middle-level best practices and create a new 7th–8th grade school, with a 6th grade to be added after the first year of operation. The district has provided funding for six teachers to meet for four days over the summer, at which time they will outline a plan and draft a calendar of meetings for the upcoming year. Ruben is one of three teachers identified to lead this configuration study, and the plan is for him to stay on as the 7th grade team leader when the new school opens.

Relationship building is much on Ruben's mind. He'll be in charge of uniting two groups of adults hailing from two schools used to seeing the other as a rival. How will he go about this? What kind of support will he get from the new principal? And what will the new principal expect from him?

CONSIDER THESE KEY IDEAS AS YOU THINK ABOUT RUBEN'S DILEMMA:

Relationships

• With any change in leadership, the culture changes. It's important to be proactive—to embrace collaboration and reach out with support and enthusiasm.

• When forging working relationships, it helps to be clear about what you believe, be flexible, and give things time.

• A change in leadership is an opportunity to define a new vision, look critically at what's working and what needs improving, and set a new course, factoring in the perspectives of all parties.

Teaching and Learning

• Teaching and learning should always be at the center of what is done at school and in teams.

• A significant portion of team time should be devoted to professional learning conversations.

OUR RESPONSE TO RUBEN:
MAKE A CHANGE TO SHARED LEADERSHIP

Strengthening relationships within a group of adults who will be working together is important for any group's success, but it's especially critical in times of change. Planning activities that will help group members learn more about each other as people and as professionals is a great start. Ruben could model his intent to emphasize collaboration by asking a teacher from the other school to partner with him in planning over the summer and addressing relationship building early on. The plan and calendar they draft together might alternate meeting sites and divide tasks, thus honoring both faculties. It might stipulate that both faculties will be called on to react to and shape the subsequent action plan.

Ruben would also be wise to acknowledge the fears, concerns, and anxieties that this large change will cause to both faculties. A discussion of the unknowns they're facing—and how the faculties might work through them together—can set a positive model for the team's subsequent functioning.

Similarly, Ruben should ask to meet for a one-on-one conversation with his new principal. During this conversation, Ruben might ask her about her vision for the school, her support for teams working together, the ways she wants to work collaboratively with her teacher leaders, and what she sees as teacher leaders' function in the school. Ruben could help shape the principal's thinking on these topics by being supportive of her vision and by urging her to involve the teacher leaders as the new school takes shape. This melding of faculties will be stressful to all, so ongoing, open conversations will be critical, as will sharing information and planning and working together.

Envisioning a High-Performing and Equitable School

According to the U.S. Department of Education Office of Educational Research and Improvement's (2001) High Performing Learning Community Project, high-performing and equitable schools embrace five core principles:

- A shared vision
- Challenging curriculum and engaged student learning
- Learning community
- Supportive organizational structures
- Proactive community relations

Interdependence is the organizing principle that links the five critical core characteristics into a cohesive whole and ensures their ongoing functionality.

Ask yourself: How developed are these five core principles in your school? What are the connections among the five? Is your school moving toward a common vision? What is your school's primary focus? Do you have supportive organizational structures to help all students succeed? What are the common beliefs at your school about how students learn? What connections are there with parents and the community? Are these connections working?

Highly effective schools don't just choose one or two of the core principles as a focus; they understand the interdependence of the five. Their approach is holistic, built around a common vision. As a starting point to begin forging this interdependence of principles, engaging the faculty in this visioning activity signals a receptivity to change. Unless you know where you are going, you will meander along and perhaps miss your desired destination.

Making Shared Leadership the Norm

School leaders engaging staff in professional conversations should strive for a set of operating norms that will help ensure interdependence is in play. An example of these norms might read as follows:

- All voices are heard.
- We operate by listening and asking probing questions.
- All faculty members are engaged in decision making, as appropriate.
- All faculty members know the goals we're working to achieve.

When operating norms like these are set in motion, the commitment to carry out the school's mission becomes a collective one, and the shared responsibility for student learning forms the foundation for shared leadership.

To encourage interdependence and shared leadership, it's essential to embrace collaboration and invite multiple voices to join the conversation. Consider the following examples of what shared leadership looks like in schools, and note how they support various core characteristics of high-performing schools and invite collaboration and multiple voices.

- Two teachers have an idea that they bring to the principal and faculty. The teachers are passionate about the idea and convinced it will have a very positive effect on teaching and learning. The principal and faculty members listen attentively to the teachers' pitch and ask them to develop the idea more fully, consider time and resources and the overall school improvement plan, and then bring an action plan to the group for consideration.
- The principal asks for staff volunteers to work with the district's math curriculum coordinator to analyze recent math test scores and bring a detailed analysis of strengths and weaknesses back to the math department. The math analysis team will recommend the kinds of support or resources they believe will strengthen students' math prowess.
- The science department has adopted a new textbook. The principal asks the department chair to bring the rest of the faculty up to speed on the new curriculum by sharing the major learning strands and soliciting comments. By engaging the entire faculty in looking at the key science topics, the principal provides support to the department chair as she guides the faculty in identifying concepts that cross curricular boundaries. These initial conversations will assist academic teams as they connect learning across departments.

• Literacy is a districtwide focus for the year. A group of teachers from different disciplines meets over the summer with the objective of pinpointing the reading comprehension strategies each will teach and monitor throughout the school year. Group members will design model lessons and assessments. The group will let the principal know how much time they'll need during the August inservice to share their materials with the rest of the faculty.

• A cross-grade group of elementary teachers decides to study student math-placement practices with the goal of suggesting modification to current grouping guidelines. They form a learning team and plan to devote a semester to researching the topic. At the semester's end, they plan to bring their research-based conclusions and best-practices recommendations to the school's leadership team for consideration. They agree to keep the principal abreast of their activities and share relevant materials and studies through regular updates.

• Three teachers, all new to the profession, are joining the faculty. The principal reviews the rookies' assignments with the rest of the teaching staff and asks who might have the interest, expertise, and time to work as a first-semester mentor. The assignment will entail two half-day, administration-led training sessions for both the mentor and new teacher prior to the start of the school year and then monthly afterschool meetings with the group of other new teachers and their mentors throughout the first semester. Beyond this, mentor teachers will spend time with their charges as needed.

In each of these examples, notice how principals multiply their effectiveness by creating the conditions and vehicles for shared leadership. Inviting a teacher or teachers to take on the responsibilities of leading a group leverages shared commitment to the collective goals. The necessary condition is that these teacher leaders have the knowledge, skills, and disposition for building strong interpersonal relationships necessary to support effective teamwork. They must be adept at creating a community of peers that can function as a resource for one another. Teachers and teacher leaders, then, are at the heart of this interdependent model's five core characteristics of effective schools.

Little (2000) puts it this way: "The target of teacher leadership is the stuff of teaching and learning" (p. 396).

In this model of interdependence and shared leadership, all staff members have a twin focus: (1) *how we work together*—relationships; and (2) *what we work on*—teaching and learning.

Teacher Leadership Structures

The building principal's responsibility is to intentionally build capacity and broaden the role of leader so the complex work of schools can be done in an organized and systematic fashion.

Regardless of the organizational structure in which teachers find themselves, the keys to success are developing "a collective sense of what is important, and why" (Senge et al., 1994, p. 299). Strong relationships are built and sustained when a team of teachers work together to ensure that instruction is tailored to improve student learning. Through collaboration, they find a common voice and can go on to set a plan with clear, common priorities. Left to their own devices, though, such groups may flounder. This is why the role of teacher leaders is so important.

Figure 1.1 lays out the three most common organizational structures found in schools today. Each structure is based on adults working together for a common purpose. Whether ongoing professional training for teachers is a critical component of the structure depends on the nature of the group and the role it plays. The PLC framework is an important tool to focus the work of a group of peers on teaching and student learning. Some schools operate with both a traditional organizational structure and PLC groups sharing the leadership voice. Others combine their functions. As you peruse this figure, note areas of similarity and overlap among the three.

Can a high school science department also be a PLC? Can a blended 5th and 6th grade group of teachers be a PLC? Can teachers belong to a traditional department or interdisciplinary team and also be members of a cross-discipline PLC team? The answer is a resounding yes! Teams of teachers who gather with a common purpose to look at improving

FIGURE 1.1	School Organizational Structures			
Structure	**Quick Definition**	**Rationale**	**Primary Focus**	**Core Ideas**
Traditional	Grade-level or single-content department structures—such as a 1st grade team or English department—led by a designated chair	Based on Dewey's model for departmentalized high schools, this is the industrial model that is still the organizational model in many schools.	Social, organization, management tasks, and curriculum connections	• Meet in collegial teams to facilitate curriculum coordination. • Organize time and students for maximum efficiency of school hours and requirements. • Work with the principal as communication conduit.
Teams	Interdisciplinary or multi-grade structure—such as a language arts/social studies group, 5th/6th grade blend, or 9th grade academy—often led by a designated team leader	Supported by research, such as that conducted by the National Middle School Association (2003, 2005). Many variations of teams exist.	Collegiality, building relationships, meeting student academic needs, curriculum coordination, and some managerial tasks	• Create small communities for learning so every student is well known by at least one adult. • Use common planning time to improve the quality and quantity of interactions between students and teachers. • Use a common vision to guide decision making as part of an expanded leadership structure. • Teach a core academic program with engaging, relevant, and integrative curriculum. • Empower teachers to make decisions.
Professional Learning Community	Framework for organizing professional development in small "communities" that fit into traditional or team structures or can be a complementary standalone structure, usually facilitated by a designated teacher leader	Developed by Rick DuFour. Various PLC models with specific protocols and strategies are available.	Professional growth for teachers with a focus on student learning, with research of best practices as the vehicle	• Ensure that students learn. • Build a culture of collaboration. • Focus on results. • Remove barriers to success. • Work hard.

teaching and learning in their classrooms over time become a community of learners. As author and researcher Rick DuFour (2004) points out, "To create a professional learning community, focus on learning rather than teaching, work collaboratively, and hold yourself accountable for results" (p. 11).

Think of the car you drive, whether it's a Ford minivan or a Honda Civic. The standard car model has four wheels propelled by a motor. The four wheels could be the departments or grade levels or interdisciplinary teams. The motor that drives them all is the principal. When all are in synch and working as expected, the wheels move in the same direction—say, toward the school's vision. In the newer, hybrid car model, those wheels are part of two interconnected, interdependent systems—one combustion, one electric—working in tandem. The combination of the systems makes the overall machine more efficient. Now, think of teacher leaders and their smaller teams of teachers as the hybrid's electric power system and the school's overall, principal-led organization as the hybrid's gasoline system. They are different, but both are propulsive and capable of moving "the whole" forward. Together both have specific roles and functions that are linked for efficiency and meet the energy demands for the 21st century. A newer, more responsive model is the result.

A good example of this newer model can be found at Sandy High School in the Oregon Trail School District at the base of Mount Hood. This comprehensive high school of about 1,500 students has a six-period day and is organized in departments. Departments manage and coordinate the curriculum and focus on student learning and support needs. A few years ago, several new faculty members at Sandy High agreed that something was missing. This small group went on to create a Critical Friends Group, using a set of guided conversation protocols to look more analytically at their own teaching practices and learning needs. Participation in the group eventually expanded to include a teacher leader.

Eventually, one small cohort within Sandy High's Critical Friends Group, troubled by the school's high dropout rate, decided to investigate the possibility of forming 9th grade "houses," or academies. The

QUESTIONS
to Consider

---→ In your school, what are the expectations for professional collaboration and relationship building?

---→ What structures are in place to focus on student learning and professional development?

idea was to divide students at this grade level into smaller learning teams and link two or three subjects in a block schedule arrangement. The rationale? Developing a stronger sense of community among and between students and teachers would help to boost student achievement, which, in turn, would reduce dropout rates. As the cohort at Sandy High conducted its investigations, they sought out others for critical conversations with regard to math placement, as math scheduling and the personnel available to teach math would be affected if smaller teams were created.

This small, voluntary professional learning community at Sandy High School grew to 8 teachers, then to 20, and is now 41 members strong. The faculty also meets in smaller groups, across departments, to look at teaching and learning from different vantage points. Two engines—the school's Critical Friends PLC and the school's traditional curricular departments—are driving Sandy High School in the same direction: toward meeting students' learning and relational needs.

ELISE'S DILEMMA

Elise is a veteran teacher leader who is now working with her fifth principal in 12 years. This principal, hired from within, is new to the position. He was formerly the school's athletic and activities vice principal. Elise wonders what his leadership style will be and whether she will be called on to perform quasi-administrative tasks as he finds his rhythm. She knows new principals often bring their own agendas. What else will she have to add to her already overloaded plate? She's concerned.

 CONSIDER THESE KEY IDEAS AS YOU THINK ABOUT ELISE'S DILEMMA:

Relationships

• Shared leadership takes many forms, and teacher leaders can influence the direction it takes.

• Teacher leaders should be ready to extend their working relationship to the principal and be part of schoolwide teams as well as smaller, more focused ones.

• A change in leadership is an opportunity to define a new vision, look critically at what's working and what needs improving, and set a new course, factoring in the perspectives of all parties.

Teaching and Learning

• Consistent "it's all about learning" messages are one way to highlight a team's core values. Having this motto visible in halls and classrooms demonstrates your commitment and alerts the administration (and students and parents, as well) to what drives your work.

• Professional learning should be defined as the center of what is done at school and in teams.

OUR RESPONSE TO ELISE: REACH OUT TO THE NEW LEADER

We would advise Elise to work on building a relationship with the new principal. She should begin by making an appointment to meet with him, and during the meeting, she should ask three questions:

1. What's your vision for the school?

2. How can we work together to support teachers and their work with students?

3. What do you see as my role as a teacher leader, and is that open for discussion?

Any change in personnel and leadership affects the whole organization. At those times, teacher leaders have a critical opportunity to influence the vision and work of the school by building support for what they believe is key to its success. So, Elise should share her dreams for the school and ask what the new principal's are. She should look for common ground and begin building there. She might consider helping her principal get started by volunteering to take on a few additional tasks, like organizing textbook checkout, setting up faculty inservice group tasks, or coordinating materials for the staff handbook revisions. This also might mean asking members of her department to give the new leader a chance and be patient with him as he gets a clearer picture of what works and what needs to change.

Shared Leadership as Conduit for Communication

As teams become the structure for teacher expression, decision making, and the consideration of best practices, the teacher leader focuses on keeping team conversations on track and ensuring active communication throughout the school community. Additionally, the teacher leader is responsible for seeing that teams' findings are circulated among all the organizational structures and that these findings make their way from team recommendation to classroom application.

Bringing a group of educators together around a common vision, where shared leadership is the norm, small learning teams are the structure, and relationships among the faculty are collaborative, provides support for the school's core function: student achievement. In this model, where teacher leadership plays an integral part, giving teachers a legitimate voice and role assumes a readiness on the part of the administration and the teachers to raft down the same river. When teachers and administrators navigate the rapids successfully, there is a sense of satisfaction, pride, and possibly exuberance in having embarked on this journey together.

Great Resources on Shared Leadership

• Leadership profile instruments can be useful and illuminating. Many are available online. Check out the Dimensions of Leadership Profile and Understanding Personal Learning Approaches (available through Inscape Publishing/Carlson Learning at www.hughescon-sultinggrp.com) and McREL's Balanced Leadership Profile, which is designed with principals and aspiring principals in mind (available at www.mcrel.org).

- The National School Reform Faculty Harmony Education Center (www.nsrfharmony.org) provides information and protocols to facilitate Critical Friends Groups. These can be useful to all kinds of teams.
- *The Fifth Discipline Fieldbook* (Senge et al., 1994) is a classic look at systems thinking. This book has a plethora of resources, exercises, and context for creating a shared vision and developing the components necessary for a healthy organization built on teams.
- *Cultivating Leadership in Schools: Connecting, People, Purpose, and Practice* (Donaldson, 2006) has useful information and tools, particularly in the section "Teacher Leaders as Partners in the Leadership Relationship" (pp. 80–86), in Figure 9.1: "Skills for the Leadership of Renewal" (p. 155), and in "Chapter 18: Critical Role of Leadership."
- *What Works in Schools: Translating Research into Action* (Marzano, 2003) is an absolute must-buy for its focus on research-based best practices to support student achievement. Especially pertinent are Chapter 18's look at the "Critical Role of Leadership" and the appendix titled "Snapshot Survey of School Effectiveness Facts," particularly the category "Collegiality and Professionalism" (p. 181).
- "What Is a 'Professional Learning Community'?" (DuFour, 2004), an article in the May 2004 issue of *Educational Leadership* (Volume 61, Issue 8), defines four big ideas that are the core principles of PLCs and provides compelling examples of each principle.

DEAR DONNA

 TEAMING WITH NEW TEACHERS

DEAR DONNA,

I have been a teacher leader for 16 years. I am finding that new teachers don't seem to need my advice, and some even question how I run the team. Any advice on how I can be more effective?

JOAN FROM PERRY

Dear Joan,

Younger teachers do need a gentle hand to guide them through new and challenging experiences. That said, most new teachers today have already had some experience working in teams. You might ask them about this as an informal, quick assessment of prior experiences. Then ask what makes them work well and what hinders (or has hindered) their effectiveness. Ask what their hopes are for being part of a team. Be sure to listen and validate each teacher's contribution.

Remember the purposes you had 16 years ago for working in teams? Share those. It's always appropriate to revisit the whys of teaming; this conversation may grow in ways you can't imagine and strengthen what you all do together. Strive to work collaboratively, and allow the newer team members space to grow in the profession and in the team.

Donna

 ## THE PRINCIPAL'S PART

DEAR DONNA,

I am a middle school principal. Our school teams are organized into PLC groups now and have been for a year. Things are going very well, but we have had a few rough spots along the way. I would really like to hear what advice you have for me, the principal, as someone who really wants to support his team leaders.

PETE FROM GARDEN HOME

Dear Pete,
A principal is the glue that holds the staff together. As the principal goes, so goes the school! I hope you are removing as much of the administrative work from your team leaders as you possibly can so that the leaders and their teams can focus on building relationships and raising student achievement.

Personally, as a teacher, I want my principal to value me and my expertise whether or not I am a designated leader. I want my principal to have a vision, help the staff to understand that vision, and then provide avenues for pursuing it. I want a principal who believes in me as a teacher, respects my talents and abilities, and encourages me to be creative and engage the students in my classroom. So when I join my team for doing the important work of analyzing teaching and learning, I want my principal to value us as a team and to support us in any way possible. Teams need inservice opportunities, resources (including time), and opportunities to join together in conversations about what is working for students and what new directions need to be taken. My principal operates like this, and our school has done amazing things for students. I am sure yours does as well.

Donna

 ## WHEN THE PRINCIPAL DOESN'T LIKE TO SHARE

DEAR DONNA,

I need your help. My principal likes being in control. We do have a leadership team in our school, but all we do during these team meetings is follow his agenda, and he tells us what he wants us to do. Now and then he asks our opinions, but not very often. I would like my leadership role to be more meaningful. Any suggestions?

HEATHER FROM BRIGHAM CITY

Dear Heather,
Sharing leadership can be scary for some people. How can your principal be invited to risk sharing leadership with teacher leaders in a way that does not diminish his sense of authority or place him in compromising situations? Perhaps he could be encouraged to focus more on managing day-by-day school operations while the teacher leaders assume more responsibility in overseeing curriculum. Adding a peer coaching program or working on cross-curriculum units within teams could be a good start. Give your principal a strong rationale for the changes, and allow him time to think about your proposal. Maybe developing a joint leadership plan will do the trick.

Donna

2

the teacher as leader

Consider the common rubber band. It isn't anything special in and of itself, but when you consider a rubber band's flexibility, its strength, and its versatility, it is remarkable. It can bind together like and unlike shapes. It comes in a variety of sizes, can be used for different purposes, and can be used over and over. If stretched too much, it can break. If stretched too often, it loses its elasticity. When functioning properly, it is almost unnoticeable. When you need one and don't have one, it's irreplaceable.

Teacher leaders, working with colleagues, are the metaphoric rubber band in effective schools. They, too, hold things together, are flexible and adaptable, and will snap if stretched too far or for too long. When teacher leaders are functioning well, they do not call attention to themselves.

But when they are absent, their absence can weaken the integrity of the overall structure.

As Barth (2001) observed, "The more educators are part of the decision making, the greater their morale, participation and commitment in carrying out the goals of the school" (p. 82). For many schools, this commitment to participation and collaboration comes about when groups of teachers are organized into teams, departments, or smaller learning groups with a leader representing each group. It's a structure that invites more voices to be part of decision making and, thus, help set the direction for the school, support what happens in the classroom, and build continuity into programs and initiatives. Teacher leaders, with their instructional skill and "way of thinking and acting that is sensitive to teachers, to teaching, and to the school culture" (Lieberman, Saxl, & Miles, 2000, p. 349), are key to maintaining the functionality of this system.

At Image Elementary School, an 800-pupil suburban school in Vancouver, Washington, a select group of teachers sits with the principal as an instructional improvement "design team." The group has a specific role: *investigating and modeling best practices to impact instruction.* The teachers on the design team are expected to learn, implement, and model new instructional practices and to engage in peer observations as one way to work closely with colleagues at their grade level. The principal understands that relationship building and a focus on best practices have the power to change a school. These teacher leaders have a voice in what happens throughout the school, emphasizing the school's culture of collaboration about teaching and learning.

For this principal, the design-team structure multiplies her reach. Now all faculty participate in high-level, relevant professional development activities led by members of their own team, not by outside professionals. This on-staff expertise has made all the difference in the eyes of fellow teachers. The principal's vision and the structures she has put in place define the nature of teacher leaders at Image Elementary School.

Thinking About Becoming a Leader of Teachers?

How one becomes a teacher leader, the criteria for the position, and the position's roles and responsibilities largely depend on how willing the school and school district are to bring teacher voices into the mix. Some district leadership models allow principals to structure the school's leadership in ways that support their individual philosophies. Principals select teachers as leaders who have the skill set that's appropriate for a given situation. Other districts have carefully spelled out, centrally organized teacher leadership models. For example, a number of years ago, Portland Public Schools, Oregon's largest school district, used a five-year National Science Foundation grant to give math and science teacher leaders a stronger voice during and after major textbook adoptions. The district selected teacher leaders from the various high school curriculum departments, trained these individuals in a facilitation model, and coached them to provide training in the new curricular content and strategies. Eventually, these individuals became the secondary school on-site department leaders in the district leadership model.

In most school districts, a variety of both formal and informal leadership opportunities exist side by side. One teacher leader may earn a stipend, while another teacher is appointed to sit on the School Advisory Council, and a third teacher volunteers to attend parent club meetings for the year. A fourth teacher might be the one person faculty members turn to for technology help. Each role has aspects of "leadership" in it, and each plays an important role in the life of the school.

The criteria for teacher leader positions vary from the general and obvious—such as a willingness to serve and a facility for working with people—to more defined criteria that identify any number of specific skills, abilities, and experiences. Here are a few examples of criteria typically listed as requirements for teacher leader positions:

- A certain number of successful years of classroom experience
- Demonstrated strong interpersonal skills

QUESTIONS *to Consider*

⇢ How do you know teacher leadership is for you?

⇢ What roles do teacher leaders currently play in your school?

⇢ What strengths or talents would you bring to a group of your colleagues?

⇢ What else do you need to know about teacher leadership before you "test the waters"?

- Proven organizational abilities
- Success in raising student achievement
- Knowledge of teaching and learning pedagogy
- An expressed interest in learning and sharing

Different leadership roles suit individual strengths and interests. In "Ten Roles for Teacher Leaders," Harrison and Killion (2007) focus on the wide range of ways in which teacher leaders support school and student success. As they note, "Because teachers can lead in a variety of ways, many teachers can serve as leaders among their peers" (p. 74). Teachers considering a team leadership role should always consider three questions:

- What types of teams does my school have?
- What skills and attributes would I need to successfully lead one of these teams?
- What supports and resources are in place to help me become a successful team leader?

Now, it's your turn. Think of a team you're a part of now or have been a part of in the past: perhaps a grade-level team, a department, a student-retention team, or a small professional learning community. What is, or was, that team's purpose? Depending on the team you're thinking of, your answer might be something like *to meet student academic and transition needs* or *to build relationships that enable all students to find purpose and relevance so they stay in school*. Maybe it's *to move all students to grade level in reading* or *to develop a vertical alignment of core concepts in math*. Defining a team's central purpose establishes the *what* of the team. It also shapes the various roles and responsibilities of the teacher leader.

KAREN'S DILEMMA

Karen wondered why she had been chosen to lead her team. She hadn't applied for this leadership position, but she'd said yes to it after several pleas from her principal, even though she wasn't entirely comfortable doing so. She wanted to know why she was chosen as the team's leader, what the principal saw as her strengths, and what role he had in mind for her as a teacher leader. Would she have his support to change how the team operated? Did she and the principal both want the same thing for her team? How would she be evaluated as a teacher leader? Did her team have any say? How should she proceed?

CONSIDER THESE KEY IDEAS AS YOU THINK ABOUT KAREN'S DILEMMA:

Relationships

- Communication with administration is essential to a teacher leader's success.
- Collegial relationships are best built on mutual respect and common goals.
- Team members must have a voice in team activities, and it's the teacher leader's responsibility to initiate these conversations.

Teaching and Learning

- Research and data should inform team conversations where appropriate.
- Teachers can build capacity through shared professional reading and follow-up discussions.
- Regardless of the roles they assume, teacher leaders shape the culture of their schools by influencing their peers' teaching and learning.

OUR RESPONSE TO KAREN: ENVISION A ROLE

New teacher leaders are often concerned about what's expected of them. This is a natural response, and it's best addressed in a straightforward manner: by going directly to the principal and asking questions. Karen should ask her principal what he sees as the team's purpose and what her leadership role is in this. Prior to the appointment with the principal, Karen should take some time to consider what she is expecting from herself. What is her vision for teams at her school? Does it differ from what she has experienced in her team in the past? What does she see as her leadership strengths? What would she want to accomplish as the teacher leader? What resources, materials, funds, and other supports would help her become that effective teacher leader?

Then, in their conversation, Karen and her principal can explore how their two visions and hopes for teams coalesce. In doing so, the principal can highlight what he sees as Karen's strengths and why she makes a good choice as the new teacher leader. This beginning conversation starts a dialogue between the two and sets the stage for ongoing communication.

Once Karen has spoken with her principal and gotten his take on her teacher leader role and the team's purpose, she needs to share these ideas and her own with the other members of her team. Their input is critical to the visioning process. Karen can go on to create *her* team (and strengthen her leadership) through listening, asking questions, staying positive, establishing traditions, and sharing the reasoning and research behind the approaches she champions. And she can increase her team's chances for success by keeping the principal informed of its progress and of the materials, time, or mentoring and coaching that will best support her work.

Roles and Responsibilities of Teacher Leaders

Once a teacher puts on the mantle of leader, that teacher is in a position to make a powerful difference in the life of the school. The roles, requirements, and attention of a teacher leader fall into four broad categories:

1. *Interpersonal coach*: Communicating, building trust, listening, encouraging, organizing, cheerleading, and providing resources.

2. *Academic facilitator*: Working side by side with colleagues to focus on teaching and learning through such activities as analyzing

data, reading about best practices, aligning curriculum, investigating and implementing new teaching strategies, creating learning opportunities, mentoring, and modeling and observing new practices.

3. *Team manager*: Organizing what's done, when, and by whom; developing systems and structures; and performing other administrative tasks, such as selecting and ordering materials and texts.

4. *Administration liaison*: Advocating, representing, and advising.

Here are a few examples of what a teacher leader typically does (notice the connections to the four categories just mentioned):

• Serves as a communication liaison between the teacher team and the building administrative team

• Gathers people and resources together, defines the tasks, and asks, "How do we get there from here?"

• Coordinates meetings with team members, students, and parents

• Participates in schoolwide decision making after collecting information from others

• Convenes curriculum development meetings to align curriculum with standards and assessment practices

• Analyzes test data

• Develops academic benchmarks and classroom management policies (such as shared expectations for student homework)

• Promotes or leads professional learning seminars

• Seeks out, reads, and shares research related to current school priorities

• Models new strategies and best practice and invites others to observe

• Mentors new teachers

• Builds networks of teacher volunteers prepared to solve problems

• Advocates for students who are not succeeding or who need to be challenged

• Celebrates accomplishments of colleagues and of students

As this list suggests, the work of teacher leaders today is quite different from more traditional concepts of teacher leaders as a kind

QUESTIONS
to Consider

···→ What do you hope to achieve as teacher leader?

···→ What goals have you set for yourself this year?

···→ What are the tasks and processes in which you would need support?

···→ To whom do you turn for professional support and guidance?

of middle management reporting to building-level administration. The new model stresses being a voice in the decision making of the school and an influence on other teachers, their relationships with one another, and the teaching and learning practices going on inside each classroom. Figure 2.1 further illustrates the paradigm shift from traditional leader, a role with quasi-administrative, "middle management" overtones, to modern team leader in an interdependent, shared-leadership environment. Of course, this concept of teacher leadership is evolving; in all likelihood, the model of it in your school or district lies somewhere on a continuum of the figure's contrasting models.

For many, the teacher leadership role has already expanded beyond traditional department organization of tasks and materials. At Lakeridge High School in Lake Oswego, Oregon, teacher leaders influence what happens inside classrooms throughout the school. Consider how veteran department chairwoman Linda Mihata turned her focus to protecting the team's professional time. The English department's meeting time had been so whittled away over the years that there was only time to complete necessary managerial tasks. Linda vigorously advocated protecting the inservice half-days and monthly department meeting times so the professional engagement her staff relishes could continue. Reading a book together, grappling with grading issues, and scoring student writing across courses to check for rigor are ways the department engages in professional conversations. Along with handling schoolwide issues affecting her team (such as copier use and budgeting for textbook purchases), Linda carves out time each month to dip their collective toes into the teaching and learning stream. Then, during the three or four half-days devoted to professional learning, the department circles back and dives into the various topics they touched on earlier in the year. Working with other departments and networking with a sister school across the lake, Linda guides her team through collegial relationship-building activities as well as critical conversations about curriculum and instruction.

FIGURE 2.1	The Teacher as Leader: A Comparison of Roles and Responsibilities	
Role	**Traditional Leadership**	**Team Leadership**
Goal Setting	Presents group members with the schoolwide goals set by the administration	Works with team members to define appropriate team subgoals within schoolwide goals
Agenda Setting	Sets agendas; may or may not distribute agendas before the meeting	Formulates agendas using input from team members
Conducting Meetings	Carries out the agenda in a formal, structured manner	May delegate or share moderation duties in a less structured, give-and-take manner
Disseminating Information	Chooses what information is shared and when	Shares all information
Taking Action	Leads action and delegates some duties; tasks are completed in the order assigned	Does not automatically assume leading role in actions; uses team expertise and strengths to guide role assignments

What Teacher Leadership Is and Isn't

A large body of research on effective teacher leadership gives us a picture of what it can and should be. According to Katzenbach and Smith (2003), high-performing team leaders share the following common characteristics. They

- Know the goal is team performance results instead of individual achievement.
- Act to clarify purpose and goals, build commitment and self confidence, strengthen the team's collective skills and approach, remove external obstacles, and create opportunities for others.
- Strike a balance between doing things themselves and letting other people do them.
- Do not have all the answers.
- Believe they cannot succeed without the combined contributions of all members of the team.

• Are not the ones in control, but balance making a decision and sharing the decision making.
• Never excuse away shortfalls in team performance.
• Encourage people to take the risks needed for growth and development.
• Work to ensure that everyone on the team does roughly equivalent amounts of work.
• Share the credits and celebrate successes. (pp. 131–132)

Your turn. Think about teacher leaders you have been privileged to work with who made a difference. What did those leaders do that made them effective, made them stand out, and made that difference?

Of course, although teacher leaders are important, significant, and vital, some teacher leaders display attitudes that can actually be detrimental to their leadership. Because of this, it is important to delineate what teacher leadership *is not*:

• A right or a lifelong entitlement
• A position from which to control others
• A way to reward favorites
• A ticket to the "in group"
• A placeholder on a resume
• Another set of eyes for evaluating a teammate's performance
• A role for which everyone is suited
• Without risk
• Always effective
• A rubber stamp or piece of window dressing

"Can I Be a Teacher Leader?"

The simple answer is yes. The more appropriate answer is yes, *if.* Yes, you can be a teacher leader *if* you meet the criteria for the role as defined by the school or the district; *if* you understand the time commitment (working with a group takes time that extends beyond the school day); *if* you are willing to enhance your own learning as you grow into the role; and *if* you believe you are able to move a group of adults forward by focusing on relationship building and teaching and learning.

High-performing teacher-led teams do not happen by accident. Working with a group of adult colleagues can be challenging because it requires careful attention to varying skill sets and experience levels and also requires a great deal of tact. Teacher leaders need a working knowledge of group-processing and communication skills, including active listening, rephrasing, asking probing or follow-up questions, moving conversations along, opening and closing meetings, managing meetings, and sharing tasks equitably.

Ask yourself: If you are not presently a teacher leader, what obstacles have kept you from pursuing the role of teacher leader? How might you remove or overcome these obstacles? What kind of help would you need, and from whom?

Teacher leader positions and roles can be as simple or as complex as the organization and members allow. For some, the role of teacher leader is an ongoing, extensive role and a very good fit. For these teachers, the relationships they build between faculty and administration, much like a well-oiled machine with cogs that fit together and move smoothly in the same direction, can transform the nature of their work and their school.

Think again of a rubber band. If it is too small for the job, it squeezes the objects it's binding tightly and leaves indentations—or it simply snaps. If the rubber band is too large, it allows the objects to move around too freely and fall out. All of this is to say *fit matters*. Some teachers are comfortable leading a specific study group or chairing a task force or committee—something with a limited, specific time commitment. Others prefer keeping their focus on the classroom. Still others may have outside commitments that are a priority. For some, the roles and responsibilities of a teacher leader are a fit. The contours and elasticity provide definition, and the work is meaningful; it's a match.

Effective teacher leaders possess a passion for teaching and learning. They exhibit a strong personal commitment to others' success, are performance oriented, and understand relationships require nurturing. They value the interests of their immediate teammates and the interests of the school, and they are willing to do what it takes to pursue both, in balance and in tandem.

TOOLS
You Can Use

···→ Tool A (p. 137) is a self-reflection exercise focused on gauging your readiness to be a teacher leader.

···→ Tool B (p. 140) is a goal development template that can help you map out your next steps in leadership development.

Great Resources on the Teacher as Leader

- *The Wisdom of Teams: Creating the High-Performance Organization* (Katzenbach & Smith, 2003) is the seminal book on the subject. We particularly recommend two sections: "Team Performance: Old Insights and New" (pp. xvii–xix) and "Team Basics" (pp. 61–64).
- *The Team Handbook: How to Use Teams to Improve Quality* (Scholtes, Joiner, & Streibel, 2003) is another fabulous, must-have resource. Check out "Chapter 2: Roles and Responsibilities" and the various online support resources available to book purchasers.
- *Group Leadership Skills: Interpersonal Process in Group Counseling and Therapy* (Chen & Rybak, 2004) is especially useful for the processing skills it introduces. Much of the book is technical and intended for therapy groups, but it does contain some valuable and highly applicable material for teacher leaders, especially "Appendix A: Basic Ground Rules."

DEAR DONNA

 DO I HAVE WHAT IT TAKES?

DEAR DONNA,

I am wondering if I might be a good leader for a group of teachers. Is there some way I can check that out before I actually apply for a leadership position?

DON FROM RENO

Dear Don,

Here are five checks you can use to assess whether or not you would be a good teacher leader. First, list what you consider to be your leadership strengths. Ask a colleague to do the same for you, and then compare your lists. What does it tell you? Second, look online for some self-analysis instruments that can help you identify your leadership qualities. Third, look at your past classroom evaluations to see if your evaluator has identified any traits in you that might be useful in a leadership position. Fourth, talk with your principal and other teacher leaders about the leadership structure in your school. See where you might fit in. Fifth, and finally, make sure you understand and support the mission and goals of your school, and ask yourself how you, as a leader, can advance that mission and those goals.

Donna

LEADING FROM OUTSIDE THE CORE CURRICULUM

DEAR DONNA,

In my school a teacher leader is both a manager of a team and team activities as well as a curriculum leader. I'm interested in teacher leadership because I love working with and motivating others, but I am a drama teacher, and I really don't know much about my school's academic program. I am wondering if I qualify to hold the position of teacher leader? What do you think?

SHARON FROM CUMMING

Dear Sharon,

Depends! Academics is the business of schools, and it is hard to lead in an area where others have more experience and expertise. However, you and your teammates might think about a shared leadership style. Depending on how the team's work is structured, you might be a very effective leader. The key for you would be to focus on the creative, motivational, and interpersonal side of the team's work and look to other members to handle the academic focus. Remember, too, that your participation on the team will help you develop academic expertise that you don't presently have.

Donna

3

building the team

Imagine for a moment you are the foreman at a construction site. Your job is to lay the foundation for a four-story brick building. As foreman, you work with a crew to level the site, adding sand and gravel for fill as needed. You outline and mark the dimensions of the structure, prepare and place forms for concrete, set rebars at correct intervals for internal support, and make calculations to determine the necessary quantities of construction materials. Once the foundation has been poured and allowed to cure, the actual brick-and-mortar work can begin.

Perhaps your construction crew is not putting up a new building but getting ready to remodel an existing one. As foreman, your first task is to determine if the foundational supports are well made and strong and if the utilities are operational and reliable. If you find cracks in the foundation, if water leaks are evident, or if electrical systems are failing, you note what structural and utility repairs must be a priority in the remodeling.

Our real concern, of course, is teacher leaders and teams under construction. In schools, the bricks are teaching and learning, and the mortar is the relationships that surround the bricks, hold them in place, and allow the school to function. Whether you are building a new team or reenergizing an existing one, before you get to the bricks-and-mortar stage, you need be sure certain foundational processes and systems are in place. These will be the internal structure that strengthens the team as it functions throughout the year. Just as the construction foreman works from a blueprint that details the building's specifications, your blueprint consists of all the routines and systems needed to support a functioning, effective team: a clear purpose, set meeting dates and times, protocols for making decisions, meeting routines and roles, systems for regular communication, team-building measures, and a defined process for setting goals. When these are in place and operational, you have a base structure that will support the work of the team.

ELISE'S DILEMMA

Elise and her team had been together for a number of years. It had gotten to the point where she did most of the work for the team. Others were always busy or didn't follow through on assignments well enough. As she started a new year, Elise hoped she could change how her team worked; she wanted team members to come together to engage in common work and to think of participation and follow-through as a matter of professional pride. She thought about asking the group to create common agreements, but this felt forced. Then she wondered if her teammates would be willing to give her feedback about what they saw as working or not working under her leadership, but that felt too risky. Elise had three days to come up with an agenda for the half-day August inservice meeting, and she was stuck.

CONSIDER THESE KEY IDEAS AS YOU THINK ABOUT ELISE'S DILEMMA:

Relationships

- A sense of shared commitment really begins when everyone feels they have a voice in a discussion and the focus for the work of the team has been defined.
- The teacher leader is in the driver's seat and must be willing not only to share his or her thoughts about leading the team and about teamwork but also to let others know as this thinking evolves or changes.
- Change takes time and is achieved in increments.

Teaching and Learning

- Teacher leaders are responsible for getting group buy-in for a common focus that is meaningful and thought provoking.
- Professional learning conversations that produce results tend to begin with a focus on data, research, a startling finding, or a compelling topic.
- Protocols are a valuable way to direct and structure professional learning conversations.

OUR RESPONSE TO ELISE: LEAD BY EXAMPLE

We'd suggest Elise start by sharing her goals, insights, and dreams with the team and go on to acknowledge her desired shift to "leader as collaborator" from her past role as "leader as executive." For her team's next meeting, Elise might engage the group in a team activity based on the triple *Ss*—shared work, shared leadership, shared responsibility—and discuss the results. If one of the team's goals is to develop a student portfolio system, for example, Elise could distribute information and research links for various portfolio systems and ask the team members to work in pairs to research the various systems. After 30 minutes of information gathering, pairs would report out on their findings, and the team as a whole would debate the merits of each system. Then Elise might call for a group vote on which system to pilot for the upcoming term. In this scenario, sharing knowledge, sharing decisions, and welcoming various perspectives all point to shared leadership and a shared responsibility to move forward as a team.

Elise should let her team know she'll be asking for their feedback throughout the year as she continues to refine her leadership skills with this new model. We would also recommend she begin a discussion about the team's goals and the activities that will be attached to those goals. Once the activities are set, the team should create a timeline for launching them and monitor the activities' effect on the team members' work with students and with one another.

As always, Elise should start the next meeting with food, warm greetings, and (if she's comfortable doing so) a fun little activity. An easy one she might try is to distribute various items or toys (e.g., a miniature kaleidoscope, a pair of chopsticks, and a box of raisins) and ask group members to explain how each item is a symbol or metaphor for the year ahead. These conversations will take the group members far and wide, generate insights into one another's thinking, and refocus them on how they might rely on one another's strengths. Elise can find plenty of similarly easy and inexpensive meeting starters and team-building ideas in student leadership manuals and cheerleader camp guides.

Ultimately, Elise will be amazed at how good things feel when her team connects and collaborates, not the least of which will be better thinking and better results. In the end, the goodwill she builds will be an invaluable boost for team learning, which will translate into increases in student learning.

Crossing the Cultural Divide

For many educators, a teacher-led team culture is something new and takes some getting used to. A culture built around sharing ideas brings both individuals' strengths and their weaknesses into the light, which involves risk and some level of discomfort. The "queen bee" syndrome doesn't fly well in this culture, and for some, going from *me* to *we* is a significant adjustment—one requiring conscious effort and focus. Of course, once teacher-led teams become the structure for the work of the school, the rewards in terms of student success, personal relationships, and job satisfaction will demonstrate that the risk was worth it.

For example, imagine you are leading a grade-level team's shift from a routine managerial focus to one centered on professional learning together. You'll need to engage in a deliberate, thoughtful examination of the relationships and workings of the team, just as if you were making a structural analysis of a building. This involves checking to see what is in place and assessing the foundation's ability to withstand the metaphorical seismic jolt of this cultural shift. You'll have to ask yourself: *Where will the cracks form?*

Think about the group of individuals who make up the team: What are the personalities and idiosyncrasies of the various individuals? How might these play out in a group setting? Think also about team communication, team meetings, and informal interactions: Are there areas that stand out as troublesome? Have you noticed rough spots or weak links, such as one person dominating meetings, another person perpetually arriving late, or another being unwilling to be part of any project? Are small cliques forming?

Often, revisiting agreements or your team's purpose can help to repair cracks and strengthen your team's foundation. A conversation at the beginning of a team meeting highlighting an area to refocus on might be all it takes, but you might also consider a more targeted kind of support, such as creating protocols for how the team will approach more contentious topics or how you will institute uniform practices without sacrificing individual autonomy in the classroom.

In any case, keep in mind that moving to a collaborative team culture takes patience and practice. The purpose of this sometimes difficult shift is to build the relations that will help teachers boost student success. For some, working and sharing with a group is not second nature. Your goal, over time, is to build team foundations so that open, respectful ways of operating emerge.

Groups come to embrace a common culture through collective discussion and ongoing conversations, ranging from explorations of what the team might be able to achieve that an individual couldn't to conversations about making a shift in how professional development activities will be done. When the time comes to kick off this process, consider doing so at a half-day, off-campus retreat. An out-of-the-ordinary activity like this emphasizes the shift in your way of conducting team business and underscores how critical these initial conversations are to building relationships and establishing team identity and culture. Moving the first meeting out of the school is also a practical way of escaping interruption while you engage in the critical work of building your team's base.

Once your team has gathered, consider beginning with these conversation starters:

1. Invite individuals to share their hopes about what the team might become and what it might achieve. Record these in a list. If necessary, prompt the group to think about how teammates might support each other and work together to promote students' academic growth.

2. Develop a T-chart listing the attributes of an "effective team" on one side and the attributes of an "ineffective team" on the other. Compare hopes about what your team might achieve with the attributes in the T-chart. Note any areas of overlap, and see if anyone has another attribute to add.

3. Brainstorm what team members might actually do to become an effective team.

4. Talk about balancing the need for individual autonomy and team interdependence. What might this look like? Play out a scenario or two for the group.

5. Identify how you see the team organizing its time (meetings, sharing students, flex scheduling, and group work, if applicable). Ask others to share their thinking.

6. Consider various roles for team members and ask individuals to volunteer their thoughts about how they might contribute.

7. Identify questions members have or want to explore at some later date, and then add those to future meeting agendas.

The idea here is to help team members gain insight into one anoth-er's perspectives, values, and beliefs. These conversations need not be completed in one session or even several sessions. At this formative stage, take as much time as feels right to develop the relationships and create the structures for operating together. Remember, these agree-ments and understandings will provide the foundation for your team's future work.

Ideally, the definition of "team" your group will generate will resem-ble this one, from Katzenbach and Smith (2003): "A team is a small number of people with complementary skills who are committed to a common purpose, performance goals, and approach for which they hold themselves mutually accountable" (p. 45). You might decide that a team is *a group of colleagues working together over time with an agreed-upon focus.*

From data analysis teams and book study groups to grade-level and core subject teams, who you are and what you are about influences how you spend your time together. Defining who you are at the front end keeps everyone on the same page and moving in the same direc-tion. As teams hone their roles and purpose for working together, their tasks and responsibilities come into focus. Let's take a closer look at what that entails.

Step 1: Establishing Common Agreements

Early on, effective teams formalize their rules of operating as a group. These ground rules, also known as *common agreements*, clarify what is expected and, at the same time, acknowledge the needs of individuals. (See Figure 3.1's effective process for developing ground rules.) Think of common agreements as the guidelines for supportive, respectful working relationships. An affinity exercise or a round of brainstorming can help members surface a myriad of topics for possible agreements. Topics to start the team's ground rules discussion might include atten-dance at meetings, promptness, absences, participation, basic conver-sational courtesies, confidentiality, and how to handle disagreements.

FIGURE 3.1	A Process for Forming Ground Rules

1. Ask everyone to write down what they need in order to work productively in a group, giving an example of one thing the facilitator needs, "To have all voices heard" or "To start and end our meetings when we say we will." (This is to help people focus on process rather than product.)

2. Each participant names one thing from his or her written list, going around in a circle, with no repeats, for as many circuits as necessary to have all the ground rules listed.

3. Ask for any clarifications needed. One person may not understand what another person has listed or may interpret the language differently.

4. If the list is VERY long—more than 10 ground rules—ask the group if some of them can be combined to make the list more manageable. Sometimes the subtle differences are important to people, so it is more important that everyone feel their needs have been honored than it is to have a short list.

5. Ask if everyone can abide by the listed ground rules. If anyone dislikes or doesn't want to comply with one of them, that ground rule should be discussed, and a decision should be made to keep it on the list with a notation of objection, to remove it, or to try it for a specific amount of time and check it again.

6. Ask if any one of the ground rules might be hard for the group to follow. If there is one or more, those ground rules should be highlighted and given attention. With time, it will become clear if they should be dropped or need significant work. Sometimes what might appear to be a difficult rule turns out not to be hard at all. "Everyone has a turn to speak" is sometimes debated, for example, with the argument that not everyone likes to talk every time an issue is raised, and others think aloud and only process well if they have the space to do that. Frequently, a system of checking in with everyone, without requiring everyone to speak, becomes a more effective ground rule.

7. While work is in progress, refer to the ground rules whenever they would help group process. If one person is dominating, for example, it is easier to refer to a ground rule that says "Take care with how often and how long you speak" than it is to ask someone directly to stop dominating the group.

8. Check in on the ground rules when reflection is done on the group's work. Note any that were not followed particularly well for attention in the next work session. Being sure they are followed, refining them, and adding or subtracting ground rules are important, as they make for smoother work and more trust within the group.

Source: Created by Marylyn Wentworth for the National School Reform Faculty (www.nsrfharmony.org). Adapted with permission.

Addressing these different topics gives each member insight into what standards others hold as important. As a general rule, limit yourselves to six or eight possible agreements; too many restrictions can stifle productive group work.

Agreements might look like this.

Because our meetings are important,

— Team members are expected to attend all meetings and be on time.
— Team members agree to listen to each other.
— Meetings will stay on topic; the leader will refocus the group if side conversations distract the meeting.
— Each member will follow through on actions that are agreed on by the team.
— Each member will contribute talents and expertise to the team; all team members will share the gift of time.

Being part of a team requires everyone to abide by the finalized set of common agreements. As leader, it's your responsibility to provide a written set of agreements to each team member. You should also plan to review the agreements at the beginning of each meeting, at least for a while. Doing so keeps the group focused and reinforces a culture of working together in a positive way. Soon, these common agreements become second nature, but make a point to review them periodically, perhaps at the beginning of the school year and again at the start of the next semester. Several sources for developing common agreements are listed in this chapter's Resources section.

Step 2: Planning the Meeting Structure

Think again of our construction metaphor. Putting up a building requires work. This work is to be completed on schedule by skilled workers, clocking in on a regular basis. For teams, the equivalent work is done in regular, focused meetings. In both scenarios, the workers have to show up on time. Establish the expectation that meeting times are protected times and that while collaboration conducted in the halls between classes or sandwiched between other duties can be a valuable bonus, it does not qualify as a regular team meeting. When "doing the team's business" is a priority, regular meetings enhance both relationships and commitments.

As the teacher leader, your role as organizer includes setting the expectations for the meeting routine. How you go about creating and distributing the agenda and the guidelines you provide on how team members can add agenda items are important. In initial team discussions, decide whether to establish the formal roles of timekeeper and recorder. Decide whether agendas and minutes will be dispersed electronically or on paper. If a paper trail is to be generated, will there be a team notebook? Where will this notebook be stored? Who will have access?

Let's take a moment to talk about minutes. Whether you are on an interdisciplinary academic team sharing a group of students, the 2nd grade team of teachers, or the high school math department, what you do as a group of adults to build interdependent relationships and a collective responsibility for teaching and learning is valuable. Sharing your work through team minutes helps keep the work of the team focused on one organizing principle: *We are about students and learning.* The principal and other team leaders should probably also be on your minutes-distribution list so that they can be aware of your team's work.

And because minutes will be shared, you'll probably want to establish guidelines for how to write the kind of minutes that will be most helpful. Using a standard template is a way to keep them succinct and to the point. It's also a good idea to review minutes before they are published to ensure they do not carry any unintended negative connotations. For example, minutes should record that "Mr. X was unable to keep his appointment" rather than "Mr. X didn't show up to support Janey." It doesn't pay to be flippant or sarcastic in minutes, as tone and intent can be easily misconstrued. Simple, brief, and factual is best.

For construction teams, regular inspections of a job site are part of doing business. For teacher leaders, evaluating your team meetings on a periodic basis is the equivalent. Make it a part of your team's operational structure to regularly solicit team members' feedback on what is working well and what needs improvement. Check the pace, flow, and tone of the meeting. Does everyone get a chance to participate?

TOOLS *You Can Use*

⋯→ Tool C (p. 141) is a template for creating a focused agenda for team meetings.

⋯→ Tool D (p. 142) is a template for taking clear and thorough meeting minutes.

Occasionally review the team's common agreements, and determine if revisions should be considered. If you believe it might be time to do so, add "common agreement review" as an agenda item for the next team meeting.

Step 3: Establishing Decision-Making Protocols

A foreman and his crew, surveying their project, make a number of decisions while construction is under way. Likewise, over the course of a school year, teacher leaders and teams make dozens of issue-related decisions. These vary with the role of the team, of course, but might include some or all of the following:

- Placing students in teams or checking class schedules for balance
- Setting up special grouping configurations for subjects like math
- Organizing and aligning interdisciplinary curriculum projects
- Establishing team days for group community service projects
- Choosing assemblies that support curriculum or team-building goals
- Choosing a peer observation protocol and timeline
- Discussing the pros and cons of a consistent response to student misbehavior
- Agreeing on criteria for an after-school study hall
- Setting up ways to share student progress reports regularly with each other to see what patterns emerge
- Emphasizing concepts and skills to target vertically throughout the department
- Modifying a duty calendar rotation
- Preparing an informational brochure for parents of gifted students

As you can see, some of these matters are very complex. It can be helpful to discuss decision-making protocol options and brainstorm examples of when each might be appropriate, as part of your initial work to establish structures for team collaboration. Here are a few decision-making strategies you might consider:

1. *Fist to Five.* This is a quick method for assessing and voting on a potential solution when a team is trying to reach consensus. Members hold up from zero to five fingers to convey their level of support for an idea or solution. Five fingers mean wholehearted support, four means agreement, three means "OK with reservations," two means "I'm not sure," and a fist means "I do not support this." After a quick scan of the room, move on to the next issue, guide the group into further discussion, ask for questions, and so on.

2. *Go/No Go.* Call to end a discussion of an issue, idea, or decision, and then ask each member to state publicly support and readiness by saying either "Go" or "No go," which indicates a degree of hesitation or that the member needs more information, training, or time before moving forward. Then ask anyone who said "No go" what it will take to move to "Go." Each no-goer then explains his or her needs or concerns.

3. *Leader's Say.* Sometimes, team members might ask you to consider input they've provided and make the decision. When a decision is made, all agree to abide by and support the decision.

4. *Ad Hoc Recommendation.* At times, a small subgroup might investigate an idea or potential decision and then bring a recommendation for action to the larger group. This saves time and allows a group to move forward with other business. This method is especially helpful when the recommendation focuses on the details and structure of a decision: for example, agreeing to the particulars in a matrix developed to teach reflection across all disciplines or agreeing to use a particular system to train students to conduct student-led conferences.

5. *Time Away.* When a critical issue comes up for decision and the group finds itself along opposite ends of a continuum after significant discussion time, if emotions are high, you might call for a limited "time away" moratorium on the topic. Everyone agrees that the issue will be revisited at the next meeting, after you've all had time to take a step back, reconsider, and see if a compromise or a different solution is possible. Additionally, this gives you time to consult with other team

QUESTIONS
to Consider

⇢ What are the advantages of teachers working in collaborative teams?

⇢ What roadblocks might be hindering the establishment or function of collaborative teams at your school?

⇢ What support or assistance will you need to help you move forward, through these barriers?

leaders for advice. The team member taking minutes should note a "time away issue" so that the decision can be put back on the table at the next meeting.

Setting Team Goals

Developing structures for collaboration is the basis for effective team-work. However, it's deciding what the team will actually do together that sets the direction for that work. With the team's purpose established, the teacher leader begins to help the group identify issues, prioritize them, and set goals. This includes specifying what group members intend to do together and what activities, resources, and timelines will guide their work. For example, is your goal to build professional relationships among teachers to support students? Is it to examine teaching and learning to support student needs? Is your goal to broaden your perspectives to define student success? Is it to provide teacher team members with support for academic best practices throughout the year? Is it to be a link between departments and teams to share knowledge about students and courses?

Keeping the two major threads of relationship building and teaching and learning for student success in mind, work with your team to draft one or two team goals that are specific and measurable. It helps enormously if the team goals also align with the school goals and with team members' personal goals, as time is always an issue.

RUBEN'S DILEMMA

As a teacher leader, Ruben swore he would never pressure anyone on his team to go along with a decision, yet one member, John, continues to balk at following through on a group agreement, undermining the entire team. Ruben hates the idea of confronting his fellow teacher, but he has heard enough rumors to know that John's "parking lot talk" threatens to sink an important project. What should Ruben do? Confront this team member, alone or in front of the group? Try to work

TOOLS
You Can Use

--→ Tool E (p. 143) is a team planning guide template, with prompts for gathering information on team interests, strengths, and current and possible resources.

--→ Tool F (p. 144) is a team improvement plan template that can help you map out intended outcomes and goal-related activities, dates, personnel, and expenses.

around him? Ruben knows he has several months before the project comes up. Should he just be patient and see what happens?

CONSIDER THESE KEY IDEAS AS YOU THINK ABOUT RUBEN'S DILEMMA:

Relationships

- The teacher leader is in the driver's seat when it comes to supporting the team's work and efforts. It's important to be generous in sharing time, ideas, and praise for what others are contributing.
- Change takes time and lots of baby steps. It requires patience.
- Teams function better when the benefits of membership are clear and there is an expectation of success.

Teaching and Learning

- Teacher leaders must be clear about the purpose of the team: a tireless focus on students and academic achievement. Everything the team of teachers does moves forward from there.
- Everyone on the team has a stake in the team's goals and action plans and commitment to address follow-through with them.
- The teacher leader checks in, both formally and informally, with individuals about their progress and acknowledges work completed or assistance needed.

OUR RESPONSE TO RUBEN: ACCEPT THE REALITIES OF THE TEAM'S WORK

The members of Ruben's team must always be aware that their team functions collectively for the good of the students. If the team has developed common agreements, Ruben should go back and review those agreements numerous times as the group coalesces. We also would advise him not to be afraid to initiate a hard conversation if someone is not holding up his or her end of the team's agreements. Waiting and hoping someone will see the light and get on board is not the answer. Ruben should arrange to meet with John privately and, at that time, invite him to share his thinking and review the team's concept and agreements. Ruben needs to let John know that he is a valued member of the team and remind him of his responsibility to the team. Does John need support to fulfill his commitment? Ruben might uncover issues, concerns, and needs in this way. If John continues to undermine the work of the team, Ruben will be obligated to share this information with the principal and ask about options for working with John.

Putting It Together

At George Middle School, a high-poverty school in Portland, Oregon, teams spent a lot of time building adult relationships to support each other as colleagues in their challenging environment. Recently, a new administrator challenged the three grade-level teams to focus their daily common planning time on exploring new ways to increase student achievement. The principal asked the teacher leaders to set team goals that would leverage both relationships and best practices for teaching and learning.

The members of the 6th grade team already had a strong affinity for one another. Its coteacher leaders felt comfortable instigating a team conversation to identify and use one another's strengths to meet the teaching and learning challenge. Team members agreed to share strategies and to practice with each other. They explored how to use data to track what they did but also agreed that data alone wouldn't tell them how to work with kids; that would involve leveraging their knowledge of their students to shape their teaching practices. Using these ideas, the team developed a set of instructional goals for the year.

To support the 6th grade team goals, the teacher leaders set out to find a program or training resource that would strengthen the data-analysis skills the team needed to move forward. A district instructional coach directed them to the Southern Regional Education Board's Learning Centered Leadership Program, which provides frameworks to guide professional development. With their team goals in draft form and with information about the cost and appropriateness of the resource to support these goals, the teacher leaders approached the principal for financial support. The principal found the funds to make training available. As a result, the entire 6th grade team has learned how to use disaggregated data to measure and document student successes and target interventions, and, in doing so, the team has progressed collectively toward its own learning goals and the school's learning goals as well.

Measuring Progress

When a construction project is nearing completion, the project supervisor readies a "punch list"—or check-off list—to compare the actual work accomplished against the contracted plan. On a punch list, you'll find all the blueprint specifications that must be met before the project is declared complete and turned over to the buyer. Tasks that are incomplete or items that have not met specification are marked for prioritization or reworking. For school teams, the way to "punch out" and ensure the team has the solid foundation it needs is to set measurable goals and assess them regularly over time.

The Team Brochure Approach

One way for a teacher leader to gauge the strengths of the team's foundation (clarity of purpose, common vision and beliefs about relationships and academic achievement, and how that translates to setting goals and working together with students) is to draft a team, grade-level, or department brochure intended for parents.

The process of creating this kind of brochure brings up key questions. Can team members concisely explain the purpose of the team, how members communicate about their work, and what impact that work has on students? Can they articulate what students are expected to learn this year, what supports are there to help students be successful, and what the standards for grades are? Do they know when parents should expect progress reports, the various ways in which student progress will be communicated, and by whom? Can team members explain the process for handling assignments when students are absent (is there a process?) and the procedures for homework and tardies? Are they prepared to address what parents can do at home to support student learning and ready to explain how and when parents can reach teachers?

If your team can draft only a portion of this brochure because you have not decided on how you'll handle each of these issues, it's a tip-off that you need to devote more time to establish your base of operations. This doesn't mean that your team is not coming together; it simply means there are unresolved items on your punch list, which can be addressed through additional focused conversations.

The Three *P*s Approach

A simple check on the three *P*s (people, purpose, and plan) can give a teacher leader useful information about how the team is functioning together and what supports or adjustments will help it achieve the intended goals:

• *Purpose: What is the team's purpose?* Ask team members to weigh in. What they say can reveal a lot about both the team's structure and how clear its focus is. How important is the team's work to members? How important is it to you?

• *People: Are members of the team building relationships with one another?* Ask members of your team to describe the team's culture and working environment. What might you all do as individuals and a group to become a more cohesive team? What do team members need from one another that they are not getting presently?

• *Plan: What are the team goals?* Ask team members to comment on the relevance of the team's goals. Are the activities, timelines, and deadlines manageable? Has the team identified the resources necessary to meet these goals? Ask, "How can I help you be successful?"

As teacher leader, check the three *P*s informally by asking team members at the close of a meeting to list on a card some of the purpose, people, or plan issues each feels need some attention. Remind your-self regularly to scan the group as they work together and assess the three *P*s. In any given period of time, you might find one or two are moving just fine while the third will have dipped. Just being aware of the three and any differences between what people say and what they actually do helps you to direct the team's focus and work more effectively.

Effective teams are established for a purpose. They survive or thrive depending on efforts made to create a safe, cohesive environ-ment. Taking the time initially to be thoughtful in coming up with the hows, whats, and whys of the group cements the individuals' "set" as a team. The resulting respectful relationships, shared norms and val-ues, and common vision and budding traditions will center the team's actions as you go forward together.

Great Resources on Building the Team

• Katzenbach and Smith's *The Wisdom of Teams* (2003) is a trea-sury of good ideas for anyone working with teams of adults. We par-ticularly recommend the Introduction's focus on the six components of effective teams (p. xxii) and "Chapter 3: Team Basics."

• "What Is a 'Professional Learning Community'?" (DuFour, 2004) is a very useful article published in *Educational Leadership* (Volume 61, Issue 8). You can access it online through www.ascd.org.

• *The Team Handbook* by Scholtes, Joiner, and Streibel (2003) pro-vides team-building tools you can put to use immediately. Check out "Chapter 3: Doing Work in Teams" for guidance on creating meeting minutes, a template for meeting evaluation, and a discussion of the affinity process. The "Meeting Skills Checklist" exercise in Appendix C is also helpful.

• The National Middle School Association's *Professional Develop-ment Kit #3: Revitalizing Teams to Improve Student Learning* (Schurr & Lounsbury, 2001) is a good guide for anyone starting a team or interested in evaluating team performance—regardless of whether you are a multigrade team at an elementary school, a core team at the middle level, or a department in a 9th grade academy. It's available through www.nmsa.org.

DEAR DONNA

 SETTING A NEW COURSE

DEAR DONNA,

I am a new teacher leader. I don't want to cause trouble, but I do want to change some things about how my team operates. Can you give me some guidelines?

HELEN FROM EUGENE

Dear Helen,

It's important to recognize what currently works in your team, what team members value, and what is negotiable. Try making a list of things team leaders have done in the past, give the list to team members, and ask them to check the top five things they would like to keep in place with you as the leader. Leave space for them to suggest other things they would like to see a new leader do. Compare the lists to see what things people value and what things they are willing to forgo. Your invitation to team members to help define a new direction in leadership is a powerful thing and will serve you all well.

Donna

 THE NEW TEACHER BLUES

DEAR DONNA,

I am so desperate! I am thinking about leaving teaching because it is so overwhelming. I am a new teacher who has three different courses to teach and a newly adopted social studies curriculum I must learn and use. Everyone on my team is experienced, and one teacher seems so knowledgeable. I admire her work, but I don't know if I can measure up. Is there any hope for me?

DIANE FROM WYNNE

Dear Diane,

The first year of teaching is the hardest, and almost all teachers struggle. Of course there is hope for you! I have three suggestions. First, set and prioritize reasonable goals, and complete them to the best of your ability. Second, seek help from that teammate you particularly admire. Ask to observe her teaching and arrive with a short list of things to observe. Discuss your findings with her. See what she does that you might emulate. Third, talk to your principal and try to arrange for the two of you to have release work time to do long-range planning and identify concepts, themes, and so forth, for your content area. You can do it. Just believe!

Donna

IT'S LIKE HERDING CATS!

DEAR DONNA,

Being a leader of a group of adults, and getting them to work together, is proving to be more difficult than teaching my 8th graders. Do you have any suggestions for where I might go for help?

HENRY FROM RAPID CITY

Dear Henry,

Go online and check out leadership ideas from groups like Critical Friends. Consult a reference librarian for resources written specifically to address the teaching or leading of adult groups. Professional associations may have leadership workshops you could attend. Finally, look at some of the teaching strategies you use with your students to see which ones might be usable for adults. Resources abound, including your principal and other leaders in your building. Someone will have an idea to share, or at least some sympathy.

Donna

4

team relationships

I n this age of accountability, school success is measured with numerical data and against state benchmarks and federal mandates. What is increasingly clear to us is that successful schools are also the ones that build solid professional and interpersonal relationships.

Go to any school and ask the children and adults you meet to tell you what makes their school successful. In her role as a school assessment consultant, Jan has asked this question many times and in many schools. Students typically respond this way:

• "The teachers, because they like each other and they like us."

• "Our teachers. They're always talking together, trying to figure out ways to make big projects part of each semester so we can show what we've learned."

• "My teacher. She helps me with problems."

• "My teachers. They expect me to learn."

- "The teachers! They expect us to graduate—no excuses—so they hound us to do our work."

When teachers are asked what makes their school successful, they often give responses like these:

- "The adults here, we all work really hard and just like each other. We have great kids here. It's like a family."
- "I think it's because of our principal, who's probably the best principal in the district. She's got a vision, and we get really energized around the programs she brings in."
- "I think we're successful because everyone here cares for these kids. No one gives up."

When prompted further, both students and teachers will mention teaching and learning as what makes their school successful, but it's the personal relationships that exist within a school that both groups gravitate to first. Relationships keep students working on a tough problem or project, make students feel visible and important, and keep teachers coming back day after day. In *Energize Your Workplace*, author Jane Dutton (2007) underscores the critical nature of relationships this way: "High quality connections contribute substantially to individuals' well-being and work performance. They also contribute significantly to an organization's capacity for collaboration, coordination, learning and adaptation" (p. 4).

The truth is, learning is hard work for both students and teachers. Encountering new skills, processes, and concepts, and then making them your own, requires attention, conscious effort, and persistence. If there is a strong relationship between the teacher and learner—when the student cares about the teacher and knows the teacher cares back—pleasing that teacher becomes important. The student is more likely to put in the time and effort necessary to learn something new, to start and finish a project, to tackle homework, and to persist even when the work is difficult.

Strong relationships among adult teammates engaged in professional learning have a similar, positive effect on what they do. The collective responsibility for reaching shared goals deepens friendships, energizes the group, and provides individuals the daily support they need to give what it takes. That synergy can mean the difference between teachers who bring creativity, innovation, energy, and patience to the classroom and those who are focused on just getting through the day.

Relationships That Support Success

In real estate, it's all about location, location, location. In schools, it's all about relationships—relationships that develop over time and are built on trust and personal connections. Teacher leaders must believe that relationships are an equal part of the student-success equation, and they must be clear that building genuine connections requires patience and ongoing attention.

Think of team relationships as a continuum:

Ineffective	Casual/Collegial	Effective and Functioning

At the low end of the continuum are *ineffective relationships*, characterized by little to no communication—or communication that is stilted, perfunctory, and without warmth. Midway along are *collegial relations,* those regular, polite, casual contacts where people exchange pleasantries and weekend-activity updates but don't make a conscious, concerted effort to connect with one another and coordinate work. On the high end of the continuum are *effective relationships*, characterized by genuine connection, sharing, and ongoing collaboration to solve problems. For teams at this level, asking advice, offering honest appraisals, and providing both professional and personal support are the norm.

Effective relationships exist when people have an affinity or connection and a basis for trusting and caring. You might characterize these relationships as *open, encouraging, two-way, purposeful,* and *fulfilling.* In an effective professional team relationship, professional strengths and weaknesses are acknowledged and, as two sides of a coin, become the basis for cooperation so that the team can be more successful overall. For instance, a teammate who has expertise as a literacy coach might offer to demonstrate two comprehension strategies in another classroom. An art teacher might pair with the math teacher to brainstorm ways to use geometry as a tool for perspective drawing. A teacher who is a genius at creating open-ended unit test questions might offer to share his approach with the team.

It is certainly the case that many faculty members within most schools have collegial relationships with one another. They greet each other, work together side by side, share social events, and have a common sense of identity as a school, a department, or a grade level. Effective teams build on that start and work with the intention of strengthening these ties. They delve more deeply into the teaching and learning practices that are happening in classrooms, identify what is working and why, and dissect what works so best practices can be implemented across disciplines. They work in tandem to reach common goals, celebrating their steps along the way. Over time, these relationships increase the team members' respect for teaching and learning and provide them with the confidence and resiliency they need to navigate change, tackle complex challenges, and sustain excellence.

Moanalua High School on the outskirts of Honolulu provides a great illustration of how relationships matter. The school's campus covers 35 acres, and its 2,000 students are spread out over seven buildings—a setup that makes it easy to understand why incoming students might feel lost in transition. To ensure this doesn't happen, the teachers and principal at Moanalua High School have set up two 9th grade teams (known as houses) to educate approximately half of the entering freshman population. Ninth graders enrolled in singleton classes, like Honors English or a higher-level math class, remain part of the regular high school and follow a standard, six-period-day schedule. All other 9th grade students join one of the two freshman houses, where a core of four academic teachers shares a group of students. The teachers in each house work to develop strong relationships with their students.

QUESTIONS
to Consider

---» Where do your team's personal and professional relationships fall on the continuum?

---» On your team, which kinds of relationships are stronger: the professional ones or the personal ones?

---» How might you go about moving either of these relationships further along the continuum?

Their goal? Ensuring that each student moves to 10th grade ready to succeed academically.

Over the 20 years that the 9th grade house model has been in effect, student success and graduation rates have increased. Today, 90 percent of all Moanalua students graduate and enroll in two- and four-year college degree programs. In short, Moanalua High School is successful because it focuses on both academics and relationships.

Assessing Team Relationships

Building a team requires deliberate attention and nurturing of relationships among team members, and for teacher leaders, that work begins with assessment. A quick inspection of the team's relationship links gives valuable information. Here are some questions you might begin with:

• Do members know each other as people and as professionals? What evidence supports this conclusion?

• Who acts as the team's encourager?

• Who always has an idea or two to share?

• Are team members able to both challenge and support one another? How do they do this?

• Who listens especially well?

• Who always comes through with solutions to tough problems?

• Do team members say (as students often do) that they look forward to coming to school on Monday morning so that they can see their friends?

The answers to these questions should prove revealing.

A more comprehensive way to assess the relationship links in the team you lead—whether it's a grade-level team, a department or interdisciplinary team, a PLC, or some other setup—is to periodically "tally the team's talk," or document what the team members are saying to one another both formally and informally. Create a tally sheet that lists the teachers' names and a number of general interactions typical of teachers working together in professional learning situations. Then, during in official team session or unofficial conversation time—say, during lunch or in halls during class changes—quietly and unobtrusively mark the tally sheet with a check or slash every time you hear a teacher making a comment or a contribution during team interactions. (See Figure 4.1 for an example.) The idea here is to make note of who does the talking and what they talk about. If possible, jot a phrase or word to provide a more detailed account of the interaction. Is it positive or negative? Respectful and conclusive? Does it reflect the team's mission of focusing teaching and learning?

A Tally the Talk assessment can give you a snapshot of the current state of team relations and effectiveness. Use the insights it generates to locate your team on the relationship continuum and guide additional relationship-building activities. Here are some conclusions you might draw from typical findings:

TOOLS *You Can Use*

···→ Tool G (p. 145) is a template for a Tally the Talk assessment grid.

• If the talk between teachers on the team is personal—about the weekend's activities, the latest TV show, headline news, last night's basketball scores, and so on—that tells you relationships are collegial and that you probably have a good foundation for development.

• If the talk leans to professional conversations about the week's assignments or homework load, field trip permission slips, or the number of e-mails from parents, you might conclude that the group is focused on managerial concerns.

• If certain team members are not talking, think about what they are not saying. Which conversations aren't they participating in? What information are they not sharing? Is there a pattern you can identify? And is this reticence typical or atypical behavior for them?

• If the talk about students and learning is characterized by frustration or impatience, attend to this promptly. Although the state of relationships is the primary focus of this exercise, you're interested in building a positive team culture, too. If the negative talk was tallied during lunchtime, at the next team meeting, you might suggest that team members challenge themselves to make lunchtime on a certain day (say, Friday) "off limits to complaints."

FIGURE 4.1   Sample Tally the Talk Relationship Assessment

Team: 9th Grade PLC   Date: Tuesday, April 12. 8:00 a.m.–1:30 p.m.   Completed by: CM

Teacher	Social/Collegial Talk	Personal Talk	Organizational Talk	General Student Talk	Learning-Focused Student Talk	Curriculum Instruction Assessment Talk	Comments
Alice	X X	X X X	X X	X at classroom. door. greets kids XXXX		XXX	working on Holocaust unit w/librarian talks about team day activities/agenda
Kevin			X		Tutoring kids at lunch	X RE: graphs/e-mail	
Greg	XXXXX Greets students, staff. talks about week activities		XXX	X X talks to kids entering room, sees girl on b-ball team		X	girls b-ball. offers lunchtime computer help inventory due. meeting agenda items? E-mail. graph skills ideas
Leslie	X		X X X lunch together team event planning	X with students at break time	X great report XXX with 3 girls/book	X X	Helps with computer checks in with librarian RE: research. meeting after school
Brian	X hellos in office to staff and others	X w/Greg	X X	X		X meeting with computer tech support RE: test results	Walk in halls. meeting later with Greg RE: team meeting

Other Notes/Comments:

– Assessment focused on 9th grade PLC team. Members are using data to analyze student literacy needs and strengthening instructional practices around literacy strategies in all content areas.

– Kevin was not out and about on this particular day. (Is this a pattern?)

– Team members overall: Nice tone with students and other adult team members!

– Greg talks with Kevin via e-mail (RE: upcoming agenda, math connections) since their rooms are in different parts of the building.

– Alice and Leslie spent time in each other's rooms discussing upcoming English unit: they're also planning to meet with the librarian together after school.

Share data you collect with the other members of the team, and consider making an analysis of these data the focus of a team meeting. Discussing these findings in this informal way reinforces the power of talk as an indicator of relationships and provides insights to chew on and digest. It might lead the team to develop a new set of goals or practices.

ELISE'S DILEMMA

Elise knew her team members respected each other as teachers. They often ate lunch together, and before school, they could be found chatting about the weekend or what they were planning to cook for dinner that night. They shared family problems and seemed to really care about each other. But they seldom spent time talking about how they taught or how they supported struggling students. Elise wanted to turn their positive relationships toward more pressing concerns of student achievement and teaching and learning, but she wasn't sure how to move conversations in these directions. How should she proceed?

 CONSIDER THESE KEY IDEAS AS YOU THINK ABOUT ELISE'S DILEMMA:

Relationships

• Teacher leaders may have to push themselves past their comfort zone in the interest of strengthening relationships and moving the group forward. Trying a new activity, bringing in a game, sharing a video clip, or doing something out of the ordinary can bring people together in a stimulating way.

Teaching and Learning

• Teacher leaders should always keep the school's vision and the team's goals visible, talk about students and the successes the team has had or seen, and ask team members to share their success stories.

• Teams should collaborate around things that matter—students' academic achievement, new curricular ideas, and more effective teaching strategies.

• A simple way for a team to measure progress is to ask, "How are we doing? What do we need to continue to move forward?"

OUR RESPONSE TO ELISE: SLOW AND EASY, FORWARD, GO

When a team boasts strong personal relationships, often small changes are all that's needed to get a new professional conversation started. Gentle prodding is the operable concept. A good option for Elise would be to share a thought-provoking video—perhaps one focused on dropout factories and city schools in crises. At a meeting, she might read aloud a particularly profound piece of student writing and prompt her teammates to share students' personal stories of overcoming adversity and finding success. She might present some of the school's test score data or attendance data and then use these to focus the team's attention on pressing student concerns. Once the conversation is under way, Elise can take various actions to keep it going: bring in experts, encourage research, maybe even identify and tackle a specific problem in a measurable way. If she and her teammates do choose to take action, we would encourage them to let their students know what the target is. As always, Elise and her team should remember their mantra: *We are about students and learning!* They'll be amazed at how quickly their collegiality turns into professional collaboration.

Relationship-Building Activities

For team leaders, it's important to be intentional about strengthening the relationship connections among the various adults on the team. It takes pointed conversations, purposeful team-building activities, group goal setting, and genuine, meaningful celebration to accomplish this.

Time is always a premium in schools, so let's turn now to some practical ideas that can kick-start the relationship-building work of teams, designed to fit naturally within a teacher's demanding schedule. Remember, relationship building is an ongoing process—one that emerges from day-to-day interactions, conversations, and personal connections. And even small interactions help connect team members as people and professional colleagues.

• Make the decision to eat lunch together one day a week. For instance, make Wednesday the "team salad for lunch day," where each person brings something to add to the lunch salad. Agree that at least on Wednesday, lunchtime is "us" time.

• Develop a team calendar that highlights special activity days, birthdays, project days, test days, and celebration events, and keep it on display so students see that you are talking, planning, and sharing together.

• Start each team meeting by reading a particularly poignant piece a student wrote or by sharing a recent comic strip or news item that connects with the theme of the month.

• Route articles or materials you come across that relate to the team's work or that team members might be interested in.

• Make sharing successes a regular cornerstone of your team meetings. Prior to the first meeting of each month, ask each team member to bring a success to share—one that has to do with reaching a student, or working though a sticky issue, or perhaps an instructional strategy that worked. Start by sharing in pairs or by table group. The goal is simply to become comfortable enough to share as a team. Through these conversations, teammates gain insights into each other as professionals.

Here are some additional ideas to consider for inservice sessions or team meetings devoted to relationship building:

• Identify and share professional strengths and skills. Explore the resources, outside affiliations, and unique previous experiences members bring to the team. Talk about how, as a team, you might leverage these areas of expertise, skills, and connections to address student learning and relationship needs. What might this look like? Consider all facets of teaching, learning, and relationship building as you answer this question: *How can we expand our working relationships and collaborate to meet whatever needs our students present?*

• List the characteristics and beliefs that unite you as a team. These might include the following: *We are passionate about teaching. We care about our students. We are optimistic and believe we can make a difference. We are committed to each other's success. We enjoy doing things with one another.* Look at the characteristics on your list and talk about how knowing who you are as a team and what you value will affect your work.

• Agree on what successful team relationships look like. Consider the relationship continuum on page 64, and talk about how your team might progress toward greater effectiveness. Perhaps you might make it a practice to find and greet each other daily. You might agree to table "school talk" at lunch once a week and, instead, talk to each other about life out of school, or you might make an award-winning novel the focus of a team book discussion. Remember, growing the team's relationships—really knowing each other and how to operate together—is important for the give and take needed to meet student needs.

• Share the results of a Tally the Talk assessment focused on observing the kinds of informal connections team members make with one another and with students throughout the day, and then share your findings with the rest of the team. Talk about patterns: Do these connections take place both inside and outside the classroom? Do team members greet each other in the hallways and walk and talk together on the way to lunch or to meetings? Do team members seek out each other over the course of a day, even if the school is large and the classrooms are in different parts of the building or school campus? Do teammates laugh together and share stories of successes, of challenges they faced, and of how they met these challenges? Do students see team members in and out of one another's classrooms, sharing materials, checking in with each other? Are all members of the team embraced and included? Discuss what this information tells the team about itself and how these kinds of connections and practices strengthen the relationship links that allow individuals and teams to know each other as people and as professionals.

• Plan a team community service project as part of your team's overall plan for a semester. Divide the various tasks associated with an off-campus experience: securing the site, collecting permission slips, lining up chaperones, ordering buses, writing a learning log for students to use on the experience, communicating with the principal and parents as well as other teams, organizing snacks, dividing students into groups with teachers and chaperones, and the like. After the event, debrief the activity by noting what went well. Did you meet your objectives? What would you do differently next time? Remember to celebrate the successes, regardless of size or importance.

What matters in any of these activities are the shared insights and the connections that they stimulate. Relationships blossom through authentic interactions, through celebrations large and small, and through conversations about who you are and why you are here. As the teacher leader, much of the responsibility for making this happen falls to you. Find what works for you and members of your team.

Working with Group Dynamics

Teachers spend their days building relationships with their students: nurturing connections and learning individual and group likes and dislikes in order to enhance student engagement in the learning challenges and tasks ahead. An effective teacher leader engages in similar relationship building with each adult member of his or her team. The teacher leader is also responsible for creating a safe environment for the group to meet and engage in meaningful work together. Regardless of the group's best intentions, negative dynamics can be set in motion that, if left unattended, will divert the team from its goals.

There are specific facilitation and communication skills and processes that help keep group interactions productive. Think back to the relationship continuum, which characterizes effective, functioning relationships as open, respectful, encouraging, and fulfilling. To help a group work at the upper end of that relationship continuum, teacher leaders need to be able to respond to group interactions, ensure effective communication, structure processes for group decision making, manage time, and motivate adults. Although these communication and facilitation skills are part of the training counselors receive, they are often absent in teacher training. Teacher leaders might turn to the building counselor or school psychologist for guidance about facilitating communication with a group of adults. There are also professional resources that can be valuable for addressing group dynamics.

Effective leaders learn to take the group's temperature during the course of a meeting, distancing themselves from the immediate group interactions in order to monitor the overall dynamic. For example, by quickly surveying body language and being attentive to the tone of various interactions, the teacher leader can tell if members are engaged, disengaged, off topic, or picking the subject to death. Heifetz and Linsky (2002) call this "achieving a balcony perspective" (p. 53), or putting personal feelings and biases aside for the benefit of the group's work.

Other group processing skills that support effective and functional meetings include learning to really listen, directing the conversation, resisting giving answers before others have a chance to contribute, keeping the meeting going, ending topics by asking for a quick summary, and noting any unfinished business. Asking open-ended questions, checking for understanding, and anticipating which agenda item might take more time or might be more sensitive than others are all part of a teacher leader's processing focus when leading a meeting.

Ease in using these group processing skills develops over time. You might begin by identifying which skills you already possess and are comfortable using along with one or two other skills that you need to work on. Ask a trusted colleague to signal you when she recognizes your effort to use a new skill and to provide you with more specific feedback after the meeting. This will help you become more adept with the skills necessary to lead your team effectively.

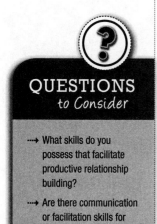

QUESTIONS *to Consider*

⟶ What skills do you possess that facilitate productive relationship building?

⟶ Are there communication or facilitation skills for which you need support?

Productive Team Meetings

Team meetings are basically social interactions. Even when all members of the team hold the same values and are focused on the same outcomes, they may occasionally disagree on ways of doing business or the work at hand. How each member communicates is important, as it influences relationships and affects the work of the group. Contrast the kind of work that can be done in a team where communication is tightly controlled and open sharing and honesty are rare with what can be achieved when all members of a team respectfully share their insights, concerns, and questions; when differences of opinion can be broached without destroying or undermining the team's relationships; and when conflicts are resolved with the genuine intent to reach a harmonious consensus rather than just to make things easier, quieter, or simpler.

Your task as a teacher leader includes maintaining a meeting environment in which all voices are welcome and legitimate, and being clear, open, and direct in your own communication and interactions. Keeping meetings respectful, on target, and within the time frame agreed to furthers the confidence your group will have in you as their leader. Meetings can be lively; there is a place for humor and lightheartedness. However, sarcasm and side conversations can easily undermine a team's best efforts, so be mindful of these and review your common agreements as needed to remind team members of the group's purpose, goals, and standards of conduct.

Based on the group interaction model generated by Chen and Rybak (2004) in *Group Leadership Skills,* we've assembled a set of sample team meeting situations that will be familiar to every teacher leader who must find ways to help team members talk to each other, challenge ideas respectfully, and bring about agreements for how everyone will work together for student success. Each includes ideas that can help you respond in ways that uphold individual dignity and further the work of the group.

1. *There are just a handful of people participating in a group decision.* To expand the conversation, you might say:

— "I want to be sure everyone who wants to can add something. _____, you kept nodding/shaking your head. What would you like to add?"

— " _____, you seem to have some reactions. Would you share? Does anyone else want to add something new before we move on?"

— "Looking at the time, we need to shift gears soon. Without rehashing what was said, any last thoughts about this topic? _____ and _____, I don't think we've heard from you yet...."

— "I'm going to move us along now—unless, _____, you have something to add?"

2. *Less vocal or assertive members of the team have not yet chimed in.* Gently bring them into the conversation:

— "Looks like you're giving this a lot of thought, _____. Would you like to share what you're thinking?"

— "I've noticed you haven't been able to squeeze into the discussion, _____. Any reactions?"

3. *A very vocal team member is continually dominating the discussion.* Intervene respectfully and with good humor:

— "_____, I'm going to interrupt you for a moment. _____ has her hand up/been trying to get a word in, so let's get her perspective."

— "Thanks, _____. Let's see what the rest of the team is thinking."

— "OK, let's go around the room. Everyone gets one brief last comment, or you can take a pass."

— "_____, let me stop you for a moment. This is an important issue and time is running out. I'd suggest we add this to next week's meeting and revisit it, then others will get time to add to our discussion. Make sense to everyone? Anyone need a second to jot down your ideas so you don't lose them before the next meeting?"

— (Say this with a smile) "_____, *not again!* Let's let _____ have a turn."

4. *A discussion has wandered off topic.* Steer it back on course:

— "We have gotten a long way away from the original issue/question! Let's get back to it now. If you have a new point to add, now's the time to speak up. Who'd like to go first?"

— "This is all good and interesting, but right now, I'm going to bring us back to the original subject."

— "Let's go back a moment to what _____ brought up. Remember, if you are just repeating or reconfirming a previous point, it's time to let another team member have the floor."

5. *The conversation has petered out.* Ask yourself if this is because everyone is considering an idea or thinking about what someone has said or because everyone has said what there is to say and is ready to move on. (Look for ready-to-move-on evidence, such as folks beginning to wrestle with papers, whisper to a neighbor, and look down at the table or around the room instead of at each other.) Get the agenda rolling again with one of these prompts:

— "Would someone summarize where we are? Then, if everyone agrees, we can go to the next issue."

— "Have we reached a decision? What is it? Who wants to summarize what we'll do?"

6. *The discussion has stopped suddenly, as if a bomb had gone off.* Quickly assess the situation and acknowledge what happened. When communication becomes uncomfortable, the silence is deafening, or people don't know what to say, intervene by saying something along these lines:

— "Boy, we've hit a sticking point. Can we look at it from another angle, or shall we put it aside for future discussion?"

— (Take a deep breath, shake your head.) "Well, that didn't work out so well. Who can help us with what's going on here?"

— "It's clear we don't all agree on this topic, but we've been together long enough that we can trust each other to find some common ground here. Shall we take a quick breather and come back to this?"

7. *Two people on a team are really at odds on an issue.* The challenge here is to keep the discussion from becoming heated and to acknowledge the legitimacy of varying perceptions. Try one of these prompts:

— "_____, can you restate your key points and then we'll have _____ do the same. I'd like for us to identify any that overlap and see if we can build from there."

— "_____ and _____, is there room here for compromise? Remember, our aim is to work together for student success; there may be a different direction or solution that will allow us to move on while still honoring your concerns."

— "I'm going to stop you two at this point and ask that the team think about the points you've brought up. And in a minute, we'll take a quick fist-to-five vote to gauge the level of support for spending more time on this issue. If everyone agrees that it's relevant to what we're doing, we'll continue to hash this out together."

8. *During a heated discussion, misunderstandings occur, feelings are hurt, and the discussion has turned toxic.* Calmly step in to diffuse the situation and refocus the group:

— "Let's take a quick break. We're bright people; I bet we can find a more respectful way of reacting and address this issue in a manner that allows differences of opinion and doesn't feel like we're walking around land mines."

— "I hear what you are both saying. We might not agree, but it's important that we all get a chance to express our points of view here. We can pinpoint the sticky issues that are of concern, but let's try to avoid reacting negatively to each other by remembering why this is an agenda item in the first place and what it has to do with helping students be successful."

9. *A meeting did not go smoothly, and one or more of the team members leaves frustrated.* Seek out each party for a private conversation, and model good conflict resolution skills:

— "I have a feeling you were really bothered by something that took place in the meeting. I'd like to understand how you felt so we can figure this out."

— "I've just had a meeting with _____, and I think the frustrations you felt may have been from a misunderstanding. Are you willing to meet and talk further?"

— "_____, as much as you might want this change to be implemented now, it is still a work in progress. I know you are disappointed. We've agreed to work together as a team so I'm asking for your patience. Here's how I'd like us to proceed.... At the next meeting, it'd be great if you had some ideas to help us as a team."

10. *There is bad news to share.* The kind of bad news teacher leaders have to share with their team is usually a message from the administration concerning something that the team wanted. When you break the news, stay positive and be clear in your message. You might frame the conversation by saying something like this:

— "We might not have made this outcome our first choice, but it's up to us to figure out how to move on from here."

— "OK, folks, I'm afraid it's back to the drawing board on our _____ idea. Let's think about how we can rework the idea with the administration's concerns in mind."

11. *A divide has developed between team members.* Despite a team leader's best efforts, minor conflicts among team members can escalate into significant divisions. If this happens, deal with the problem directly and neutrally:

— "I think we need to acknowledge our situation here and figure out how we can get back into balance as a team. Here's what I'd like to suggest...."

— "Our ongoing disagreement about this issue has started to affect our relationships and our work. I'm concerned about how we treat each other when we disagree. This is something we need to discuss, and I think we should begin by taking a look at our team's ground rules…."

Intentionally laying the groundwork for productive conversations can prevent problems and misunderstandings before they occur. If people are honest, disagreements will naturally arise over the course of these conversations. It is fine to disagree, so long as the disagreement is expressed respectfully and is focused on the issue and not another person. When conversations and discussions are tough, remind yourself to be fair, be patient, and keep frustration out of your voice. Model for your team that wrestling with issues or ideas respectfully is "the way we do business." Remember to thank your team often for their hard work and dedication. It's all of you together who make it work.

Unlike honest disagreement, conflict is a destabilizing force on teams. Thinking through the agenda ahead of time and considering what you know about the members of your team can go a long way toward minimizing conflict. If you anticipate that an agenda item might be particularly contentious, try rehearsing your responses in advance, seek a colleague's advice prior to the meeting, or build a structure that allows both sides to speak openly and respectfully.

When conflict arises, always take a moment to step back and observe the dynamics within the group. Consider the tone of what's being said as well as the words and the subject matter. Then decide on an appropriate response.

If an issue cannot be resolved, if you have done all you can to avoid negativity, and if the conflict is impeding the work of the team, do check in with the principal or others in similar leadership roles and ask for their support and advice. Sometimes just having another perspective opens up new possibilities in working through concerns. It is a rare circumstance that warrants administrative intervention, but continued instances of sabotage or unprofessional behavior become a personnel issue, which *is* the administration's concern. Facilitating team communication to enhance professional relationships and professional outcomes is part of your job, but being a therapist or personal counselor is not.

Congratulating and Celebrating

Although many teams have mechanisms in place to recognize student success, sometimes they overlook the importance of acknowledging—and celebrating—their own continued efforts and accomplishments. After all, teamwork is a process; it requires nurturing and ongoing attention.

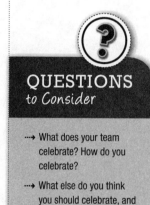

QUESTIONS *to Consider*

⟶ What does your team celebrate? How do you celebrate?

⟶ What else do you think you should celebrate, and why?

As in the larger school community, teams generally celebrate members' birthdays, babies, and weddings, and they participate in Staff Appreciation Week and end-of-the-year activities. What else might a team celebrate to reinforce its values and vision, strengthen teammates' relationships, and build a more positive culture? Here are few ideas:

• *Celebrate new skills and achievements.* Regularly ask team members to "bring and brag"—demonstrate some new instructional technique or tell a story about a team member's accomplishment with a student or a unit of study—to a round of applause. Another slightly more raucous idea that involves the whole faculty is to have a paper "snowball share." At a mid-January faculty inservice session or meeting, everyone writes one achievement on a scrap of paper—his or her own or a teammate's—identifying the who, what, and when. All wad up their papers and throw them at each other. Then individuals pick up the nearest "snowball" and take turns reading them aloud. In this way, different teams hear what's happening on the other teams in the school and share in the celebration of those successes.

• *Celebrate fortitude.* Do something nice to recognize a teammate's successful completion of a difficult week. Forward a copy of a favorite inspirational story or poem, send a note of congratulations, or bring in one of your teammate's favorite things: a flower, a collectible, a snack. This is a small way to make a difference.

- *Celebrate progress toward goals.* After evaluating the team's goals at midyear, note progress and celebrate with sparkling cider and banners for all to see. Do this in January, again in April, and in June.

- *Celebrate goals met.* Meeting an established goal—such as reaching 95-percent student attendance for a month or 97-percent parent participation in student-led parent conferences—calls for a celebration involving all the involved parties. Some ideas include holding a staff-versus-students basketball game or Ping-Pong tournament, or an evening assembly featuring a student or faculty garage band.

- *Celebrate professional development and achievements.* These range from major (such as recognizing a teammate who has completed a master's program with a party or team-purchased gift certificate) to minor (greeting the return of teammates who attended a professional growth seminar with a storm of celebratory soap bubbles) and can hit various notes in between.

- *Celebrate a successful year.* Hold a miniconference for the entire faculty at which each team highlights the work done that year in a manner of its choosing: a PowerPoint presentation, a reflective writing piece, a storyboard, or a journal article.

- *Celebrate professional generosity.* Recognize colleagues who volunteer to mentor others or to be observed or videotaped modeling a new strategy for the purpose of professional development. Teammates who have a regular planning period or duty-free time might donate it to that colleague and step in as a substitute so that he or she can have some extra preparation time.

- *Celebrate special projects completed.* Recognize the completion of extended projects, such as a team's interdisciplinary unit, by writing a story for the school Web site or the local newspaper, complete with pictures of the teachers with their students. Consider inviting your superintendent and other district office personnel to come for a "walkabout" at which students can display their work and share their learning. Make it a real celebration with punch, cookies, and written invitations, and be sure to acknowledge the teachers involved with banners and corsages or boutonnieres.

- *Celebrate "teamness" all year long.* Working as a team is not always easy, but it is always important. Recognize the support team members provide one another by reinforcing those relationships, and acknowledge working hard together in small ways with sincere thank-yous and the occasional small, token gift quietly placed in the team member's mailbox. Or go for the gusto in bigger ways. Try "Secret Pals Week" and themed potlucks and dessert parties during grading weeks. Establish quarterly "Giving Exchanges," where everyone brings books, DVDs, CDs, and magazines to the team room to be given away. As teacher leader, you might contact businesses in your area or the PTA to see if small donations of gift cards or ice cream or book gift certificates are available to pass out as recognition for those little something extras you notice or hear about. "Thank you," "You made a difference," and "Your work/effort/ideas are important" are words that should be used whenever they apply.

RUBEN'S DILEMMA

In an effort to build team relationships, Ruben asked his team to discuss ideas for something they might do to celebrate their hard work together. One team member said he was not interested in anything that would take up his time after school; he had other obligations. Several others really wanted to form a bowling team and argued for 100-percent team member participation. This idea did not meet with 100-percent team approval.

Now Ruben was in a bind. How could he honor the idea of celebrations and team spirit while still being inclusive and not alienating anyone?

CONSIDER THESE KEY IDEAS AS YOU THINK ABOUT RUBEN'S DILEMMA:

Relationships

• Getting together socially has merit, but it does not serve the same purpose as the celebration of accomplishments.

• All team members should participate in discussions of and deliberations about both social team-building activities and the celebration of success.

• Team members should acknowledge one another's accomplishments, both large and small, on a regular basis.

Teaching and Learning

• The team's vision, mission, and goals should always be a priority.

• Teams must celebrate things that matter: student success and the ideas and strategies that will boost student success.

• Adult achievements that support teaching and learning matter, too—and deserve to celebrated.

OUR RESPONSE TO RUBEN: CELEBRATIONS COME IN A VARIETY OF FORMS

Not everyone wants to spend time together outside the school environment or school day. We'd advise Ruben to hold fast to the idea of celebrating as a team but focus on authentic accomplishments and perhaps modify his expectations a bit. He might begin by reviewing the variety of celebration occasions and activities in this section of the book and suggesting a few that can be conducted during the school day. We would recommend he ask his team to discuss which of those options would be most meaningful for them, and then take it from there. And those teachers who want to form a bowling team or otherwise get together socially should go ahead and do so!

Great Resources on Team Relationships

- *Cultivating Leadership in Schools: Connecting People, Purpose, and Practice* (Donaldson, 2006) nicely addresses the human aspect of schooling. We particularly recommend "Chapter 5: Relationship Building" and "Chapter 8: Put Relationships at the Center."

- *Leadership on the Line: Staying Alive Through the Dangers of Leading* (Heifetz & Linksy, 2002) has some very valuable lessons for team leaders. The balcony metaphor in Chapter 3 alone is well worth the price of this book!

- The chapter called "Dealing with Conflict" in *The Team Handbook* (Scholtes et al., 2003) includes strong advice on common problems that are applicable to teacher teams.

- Jan's own book *A Smart Start for Professional Development: From Sticky Notes to Dragon Boats* (Burgess, 2008) provides a plethora of ideas to jumpstart team building with activities that become the symbols or metaphors for a new school year. For instance, if your team's goal is to strengthen student reflective writing practices, you might kick off the first meeting of the school year by handing out small mirrors (a symbol) and a writing prompt (writing helps crystallize thinking) that asks faculty to think critically about how they learn and process. The activities in this book are suitable for teams of any sort and at all levels, from elementary through high school and beyond.

DEAR DONNA

 STRUGGLING WITH A WEAK LINK

DEAR DONNA,

There is a person on my team I don't think is a good teacher. Kids complain about him all of the time. Short of getting him off the team, what would you suggest I do?

LAURA IN FAIRFAX

Dear Laura,

Helping a struggling teacher is important to the work of the entire team. Look objectively at what is happening on your team to see if this teacher is being included in team conversations about teaching and learning. Look to see if the teacher's ideas and experiences are being valued by the team. Are you all working with and accepting this person as an important member of your team? If there are problems in these areas, it's up to you to address them and to work toward including this teacher in ways that are validating and supportive.

If you feel everything is in order on your team, then it is time to take a closer look at the complaints students have about this teacher. Are they valid? If so, you might approach the teacher with the information you have and offer to work together to identify and address the students' concerns. Narrow the issues, develop a plan together (if asked) for addressing them, and be a positive mentor.

Although your role is to build relationships and maintain an effective team that will further student learning, do remember you are not this teacher's evaluator; the principal has that responsibility. If the principal needs to become involved, perhaps the three of you could work together to identify the areas where your support would be beneficial. The key here is to respect the line between the team leader's role and the principal's responsibility.

Donna

 ## WHEN TEAMMATES CLASH

DEAR DONNA,

Today my team meeting turned combative, with two team members at each other's throats over an issue we were discussing. I was caught off guard, and I didn't handle the situation well at all. Do you have any suggestions on how I can work with these two people to resolve this crisis before our next meeting?

DAN IN ATLANTA

Dear Dan,
Meet with each team member individually and listen to each member's point of view. Try to identify common ground in their views before suggesting that all three of you meet to talk over the recent conflict. In this meeting, be sure to validate their differing points of view, but be clear that your team *must* move beyond disagreements and into the realm of solutions. Then, at the next team meeting, remind the team that you are a team and that disagreements and conflict are natural: You aren't all going to agree on everything. What is important is to work through issues so that relationships remain intact and you can continue your efforts to support student learning. Sometimes that means compromising, and sometimes it means dropping a topic altogether.

For a teacher leader, it's often easier to manage organizational tasks than the interpersonal ones, but both are important roles in leading teams.

Donna

 ## TRUST AND OPENNESS

DEAR DONNA,

Each of our team members contributes $25 a year to be used for various socials and celebrations. The teacher in charge of the money is spending way too much on some people and events and too little on other things. It is starting to feel uncomfortable. How can I bring the issue before the team without hurting her feelings?

MAX FROM STAYTON

Dear Max,
Here, it's important for your team to agree on a basic spending plan or philosophy for using the team's money. Ask the teacher in charge of it to prepare a budget for expenditures and place the budget on the team's agenda for discussion. Agree on types of acknowledgments and dollar amounts. Lines of communication need to be opened and expenditures presented at each team meeting so that all team members know where the money is going. Do validate the past work of the teacher, and in the future, let the budget be the focus and not her past work.

Donna

5

strengthening professional practice

At the heart of schooling is teaching and learning. Both activities are highly personal. Both are dependent on individual understanding, skills, talent, and disposition. The teacher and students are like partners in a dance. Each brings past experience, knowledge, and receptivity to the other. The teacher leads—presenting ideas, concepts, activities, and expectations and adapting them as necessary to challenge each student. The student in this partnership might stumble at first but will progress with support. As the trust and understanding that develop between the teacher and the learner become part of the rhythm of their dance, teaching becomes stronger, and learning soars.

Dancing as a Team

Learning to dance well requires a competent and skilled instructor. In school teams, it's the teacher leader who ensures this instruction is available—by providing it personally or by going outside the team to find it. The teacher leader also functions as a choreographer, guiding the team into the second critical focus of its work: improving instructional practices so all students experience success. The teacher-led team begins with basic steps and builds a repertoire suited to the team's particular talents and specific goals. Then, together, they add more complex maneuvers. In other words, a team that is developing professional learning capacity together starts where its members are, sets goals, and undertakes more complex challenges as their skills grow.

Margaret Wheatley (2000) reminds us that "the target of teacher leadership is the stuff of teaching and learning: teachers' choices about curriculum, instruction, how students are helped to learn, and how their progress is judged and rewarded" (p. 340). Similarly, researcher Judith Warren Little (2000) points out that "teachers who lead leave their mark on teaching. By their presence and their performance, they change how other teachers think about, plan for, and conduct their work with students" (p. 396).

Effective teacher leaders know that as the team moves in step together—collaborating meaningfully to discuss and decide how to improve their professional practice—this collective work increases individual capacity. The group examines "what is" and builds toward "what might be," with the teacher leader designating time on team meeting agendas to engage in professional learning conversations and explore the expertise each team member brings to the group. Although the teacher leader proposes ways in which the team might collectively strengthen their practice and address students' learning needs, his or her role here is to function as a facilitator and participant—and not as *the* expert with all the answers.

Because professional learning conversations go beyond collegiality and straight to the heart of which strategies, skills, structures, and practices different teachers use, team relationships, built intentionally, must be in place to support these highly personal interactions. Opening the doors of one's classroom is a risky business, both literally and metaphorically. Our advice to team members is to take this slow, acknowledge the challenges associated with inviting others to look at your practices, and applaud each step so that sharing, asking for feedback, posing questions, and saying "That doesn't make sense" feels safe and is supported.

Remember, all teams start at different places when they move into conversations about teaching and learning. If this is a new direction for your team, consider filling out a team resource and interest map, like the one in Figure 5.1. Developing the interest map together is really a secondary goal; the primary objective is to dive in and begin talking about strengthening professional practice. As the teacher leader, be honest about your team's readiness, and don't push your members toward the tango when a simple line dance would be more appropriate.

Consider the various ways that these four school-based teams began choreographing the movements and steps that would become the basis for their professional learning dance:

TOOLS *You Can Use*

⇢ Tool H (p. 146) is a template for a team resource and interest map.

• In 2006, when professional learning teams were first introduced at Neah-Kah-Nie High School, a 400-student public high school on the Oregon coast, Critical Friends protocols helped guide cross-curricular teams' discussion and consideration of the concepts presented in Grant Wiggins and Jay McTighe's book *Understanding by Design* (2005).

• At Image Elementary School in Vancouver, Washington, team-based professional learning began with a small teacher group investigating the Reading Workshop Model together. The team read Debbie Miller's *Reading with Meaning* (2002) before attending a workshop Miller led.

• At George Middle School in Portland, the faculty read *Courageous Conversations About Race: A Field Guide for Achieving Equity in Schools* by Glen Singleton and Curtis Linton (2005). Teams used this book as a catalyst for examining their current practices.

FIGURE 5.1	Sample Team Resource and Interest Map

What We Do Well: Effective Strategies and Methods

- Direct instruction (Tess, Molly, Arturo) reading, writing, math
- Small-group work (all)
- Paired work (all)
- Investigative labs (Ryan, Devin) science
- Work with manipulatives (Devin, Arturo)
- Match state standards with our course curriculum (Connie, Tess, Arturo)

What We Read Professionally: Education-Focused Reading over the Past 9 Months

- <u>Educational Leadership</u> from ASCD (Tess/reading, Molly/writing, Connie/leadership)
- Journals and research summaries from the National Association of Secondary School Principals and the National Middle School Association (Cathie/6th graders, Connie/parents)
- <u>Science Journal</u> (Ryan/lab ideas)
- Education content in the <u>New York Times</u> (Connie)
- Stiggins on assessment (Devin, Tess/formative assessment as team leaders)

What We Would Like to Investigate: Strategies and Methods, Books, Research

- Best ways to offer students choice in assignments and exams (All)
- Differentiation in middle school English and mathematics classrooms (Cathie/6th grade team)
- PE lifetime skills games (6th grade team for outdoor school)
- Ways to engage reluctant learners (All!!)
- How to develop authentic assessments for multiple units (All, to some degree)

Actions We Might Take

- Read together Stiggins et al.'s <u>Assessment for Learning</u>
- Observe outstanding practices in another school for differentiation/assignment choices
- Find research on how to reach all readers and then investigate places where these practices are working (target reluctant and those two grade levels below)
- Watch a DVD on portfolio assessment, practice together, and perhaps design our own model to implement later in the year (add as potential goal if we read the Stiggins book)
- Talk with someone who knows how to design conceptual labs in science that students investigate (Ryan)

• The English department at Lakeridge High School read Beth Graham and Kevin Fahey's 1999 *Educational Leadership* article, "School Leaders Look at Student Work," to guide their foray into professional learning conversations.

Regardless of whether your team starts by aligning the curriculum, by participating in schoolwide training in an inquiry-based critical thinking approach, by reading a book together, or by identifying key ideas and big questions for interdisciplinary connections, keep this organizing principle in mind: *The reason for teams to examine their practices, strengthen some, and add others to their repertoire is so that they can positively affect student learning.*

Pursuing a Professional Learning Focus

If the target for your team's professional learning is not immediately obvious, taking stock of the team's current interests, resident levels of expertise, and common training needs can be a great help. Consider using Tool E (p. 143) and Tool H (p. 146) to guide these efforts. Or you might begin your efforts to select a learning goal by asking teachers to consider recent achievement test results. Do these spark any ideas for future investigation? Can you think of a goal that will complement the school's comprehensive instructional improvement goals for the year? Team members might look for ideas in various professional journals or review short research synopses of best practices in a relevant curricular area. Other ideas include examining data on the dropout crises available from America's Promise Alliance (www.americaspromise. org); looking at the Programme for International Student Assessment (PISA) comparisons of the reading, math, and science achievement of 15-year-olds across 90 developing countries, documented in the Organisation for Economic Cooperation and Development's Executive Summary (www.pisa.oecd.org); or considering the Asia Society's international schools graduation standards (www.asiasociety.org). All this information is riveting and will certainly move your team into deep discussion of teaching strategies and learning options that are 21st-century graduation targets.

As your team considers the array of goal options, remember it's better to do one thing well than to begin four initiatives that might be done poorly. The learning goal you decide to pursue must resonate with the team; group commitment is key. All members will be devoting considerable time to the goal's pursuit, so be sure you ask and answer these critical questions:

- How will this learning goal lead to improved student achievement?
- Will it improve our professional practice?
- What amount of effort will be required to pursue and achieve this learning goal?
- What resources and support will we need?
- What specifically will we commit to doing? By when?

Use the answers to these questions to finalize your selected goal and develop an action plan, complete with assigned tasks and timelines for checking in with each other. As the action plan is being drafted, communicate often and share the drafts so everyone knows what to expect. Professional learning to improve instructional practice requires teachers to take an honest and critical look at what they're doing. However, everyone should understand that the team will be functioning as a support system and not as a forum for individual evaluation or judgment. Such agreements put the structure for examining teaching and learning practices in place so no one will be surprised as the process unfolds.

RUBEN'S DILEMMA

Reading across the curriculum was the school goal, and Ruben thought his team might use that goal to begin working together as teachers in a learning community. (Usually, their team conversations focused on more specific matters, such as which student wasn't performing or who was causing trouble.) When Ruben presented this idea to his team, he got some resistance from both the math and PE teachers, who pointed out that reading wasn't one of their course requirements.

Ruben tried several arguments and appealed to their team commitment, all to no avail. What should he try next?

CONSIDER THESE KEY IDEAS AS YOU THINK ABOUT RUBEN'S DILEMMA:

Relationships

- All team members are responsible for student achievement and must commit to working collaboratively.
- Teacher leaders need support sometimes, too. Those who need help sorting out their concerns in a nonjudgmental way should not be afraid to seek the advice of an administrator or another teacher leader.

Teaching and Learning

- Reflecting, sharing best practices, and investigating new ways to address student learning needs should be at the top of every team's agenda.
- It's important to monitor the team's progress and make adjustments as needed to reach all students.

OUR RESPONSE TO RUBEN: YOU'RE ALL IN THIS TOGETHER

Because reading across the curriculum is a schoolwide goal rather than just his team's goal, Ruben might call on the principal's leadership to help bring everyone to the table. He also might look for examples of successful applications across content areas and share these with the two reluctant teachers. As a team, perhaps the teachers could develop a meaningful, relevant interdisciplinary project that had a strong reading strategies component for which every teacher assumes responsibility. It is clear that research and best practices support teaching reading strategies across the curriculum, even through high school. This doesn't mean all content teachers must be reading specialists; however, all teachers must be able to help students access the information in their textbooks and understand the content. Find materials that support this argument, and go back to the notion of collective responsibility: No one gets to opt out.

Professional Learning as a Team Practice

The actual practice of learning together as a team begins with professional dialogue focused on the learning needs of the team's students. Team members look at student performance, their own performance, areas of current problems, instructional strategies, or techniques that are not measuring up. Then, together, they identify instructional improvement goals or targets. From here, their professional learning follows a common growth model: Investigate best practices to increase student achievement; study, learn, and train together (relying on one another's expertise, trained consultants, and DVD examples); begin using new practices in the classroom; and come together frequently as a small group to discuss and dissect piloted practices.

This can be messy work. First forays with new strategies often are less than ideal, but that's the point. Talking about your practice, listening to one another's stories, reflecting on what you are learning, refining your approach, and then trying the strategy or practice a second and third time solidify both your understanding of it and your comfort using it. This cycle of *learning/using/reflecting/refining* defines professional learning as a team.

There are multiple entry points in this approach to professional learning:

• A team might ask one or two members to pilot a new practice or strategy and report back to the rest of the group.

• A team member trained to use a new system or practice might offer to train others during team meeting time and use footage from her own classroom for illustration.

• Team members who attended an after-school Web seminar might each agree to try out a specific strategy for one month, at which time they will all report back and share student artifacts.

A key to the success of professional learning as a team is using this focus to ground the work of the team's members. Always remember that relationships are built around finding ways to help all students become successful learners. Engaging as a small group of professionals using the learning/using/reflecting/refining cycle to strengthen practices in classrooms is invigorating and validates teachers as professionals.

A teacher leader's responsibilities in the team's professional growth correspond to both the interpersonal coach and academic facilitator roles. What's essential is that the group makes a commitment to learn together and keeps that study central to its work time. For some individuals, a move to learn new practices or skills collaboratively and share professionally together is not immediately comfortable. Using structured protocols, like those outlined in Figure 5.2, can help ease your team into this important work.

At Oregon Episcopal School, a private K–12 college-prep day school in the green hills of Portland, Oregon, the high school science department, under the guidance of their department head, took on the gargantuan task of presenting the various science course curricula in a Web-based curriculum map that would be available to students and parents. But before they could produce the map, this collection of independent, very capable teachers with a great deal of content-specific expertise had to focus on curricular alignment, which meant meeting and working as a single, interconnected team. Having courageous conversations about what they were teaching and what students were actually learning (or needed to relearn from one course to the next) was quite an undertaking, but it was one that the teachers felt was necessary to clarify their instructional practices and make their science program's curricula and expectations transparent.

As the team's work continued, these conversations moved beyond what was in the text of any one particular course to tackle big questions: What was scientific thinking? How could research be nurtured? What were "high standards of quality"? Which scientific concepts should students master at each level, and which concepts could be enhanced or intensified through revised learning activities? Out of these complex conversations came a group agreement that 25 percent

QUESTIONS
to Consider

- → How comfortable is your team talking about teaching and learning?

- → How much of the team's time is devoted to professional growth?

- → How much of the team's meeting time is centered on discussion of teaching and learning?

FIGURE 5.2	Sample Protocols for Professional Learning Conversations

Save the Last Word for Me *Total time:* 30 minutes

Purpose: To clarify and deepen our thinking about an issue we have read about.

Preparation: All team members arrive at the meeting prepared to discuss an agreed-upon article, research report, or book.

Setup: The team breaks into small groups of four, with one person serving as a timekeeper. Each round should last approximately seven minutes.

Process:

1. Each participant silently identifies what he or she considers to be the most significant idea addressed in the reading.

2. When the group is ready, a volunteer member identifies the point in the reading that he has found to be most significant and reads it out loud to the group. The first person says nothing about why he chose that particular point.

3. Each of the other three participants has *exactly one minute* to respond to that idea.

4. The first participant then has *three minutes* to state why he identified his point as the most significant and to respond to his colleagues' comments.

5. This pattern repeats until all four members of the group have had a chance to have "the last word."

6. The full team reassembles to debrief the experience: Was this a useful way to explore the ideas in the text and to explore our own thinking? If so, why? If not, why not?

Chalk Talk *Total time:* 10 minutes, plus follow-up discussion

Purpose: To generate, develop, and reflect on ideas as a collaborative group.

Preparation: Required material includes a blackboard/whiteboard or poster paper and chalk/markers.

Setup: Several markers or pieces of chalk are laid out before a whiteboard or blackboard. The activity's facilitator reminds the group that Chalk Talk is a silent activity. No talking is permitted.

Process:

1. The facilitator writes a relevant question, term, or topic in a circle on the board and then calls for two or three volunteers to begin the activity.

2. While the rest of the group observe silently, the first volunteers draw a connecting line from the starting idea and then add their thoughts or comments. They write what they feel moved to write and then put the chalk down.

3. Anyone else with an idea, thought, or question picks up the chalk and adds to the board.

4. The facilitator continues to guide the activity by writing on the board: posing a question by someone's summing, adding additional reflection on an idea, and connecting interesting ideas or comments together with a line and a question mark.

5. When no one adds anything over a period of one or two minutes, the facilitator signals the activity's impending close by asking, "Are there any more additions?"

6. The facilitator verbally summarizes the silent conversation documented in the web, noting themes, connections, and questions.

Follow the activity with a discussion of the ideas and questions generated.

Source: The Save the Last Word for Me protocol is from National School Reform Faculty (NSRF) Harmony Education Center, developed by Patricia Averette and adapted here with permission. The Chalk Talk protocol was adapted for NSRF by Marylyn Wentworth, based on the work of Hinton Smith, Foxfire Fund, and adapted here with permission. Additional protocols for effective team work are available at www.nsrfharmony.org/protocol/search.html.

of the science grade in all courses would involve students engaging in year-long authentic research projects. The teachers decided their students had to be able to use the knowledge and skills acquired in class in ways that showed critical thinking, and they had to be able to synthesize concepts and apply them to new situations.

In this way, the goal of creating an online curriculum map became the framework these science teachers used to engage in meaningful, relevant conversations over an extended period of time. Respect among team members for the work and expertise each brought to the department grew throughout the process. Ultimately, they arrived at a set of clear learning objectives, new cutting-edge strategies for teaching science, and a focus on quality research standards in the various fields.

The online curriculum map the upper-school science teachers at Oregon Episcopal ultimately produced only tells part of their team's story. The other half of it played out in the deeply engaging conversations sustained over time through the guidance of the team's teacher leader, the department head. This team's teaching and learning focus was not an easy or quick undertaking, but it was unquestionably valuable and ultimately created a curriculum articulation that today helps produce some of the best student scientists in the region.

In another example, teachers in the English department at Lakeridge High School began their team's year by setting professional learning goals together. Their department meeting agenda (see Figure 5.3) was designed to facilitate active dialogue that would lead to a year-long action plan for professional growth. This group of teachers has been working together for several years and looking deeply into current practices to pinpoint areas for alignment, enhancement, and consideration as part of the way they do business.

Learning from the Gold Standard

Moanalua High School has developed a professional learning structure that has been widely recognized as the gold standard model for how a large, ethnically diverse urban high school can undertake professional learning to improve instruction and student achievement. It's a height the school's staff reached after many of years of deliberate effort.

In 2000, the 130 teachers at Moanalua created a series of small professional learning circles as a vehicle to improve student learning and provide job-embedded, needs-based professional development.

Teachers fill out a self-survey each year (see Figure 5.4) indicating areas of their practice that they are interested in strengthening. Moanalua's teacher leadership team and administrators then meet to group teachers into common learning teams. Teacher leaders are each assigned a group to support over the course of the year.

FIGURE 5.3	Sample Planning Meeting Agenda

English Department Meeting:
Room 6, 3 p.m.–4:00 p.m.

We will discuss the following topics and begin narrowing our group focus for this year's professional learning. Come prepared to share, voice your opinion, and think about the hows, whens, whys, and whos; then we'll begin drafting the logistics of the year ahead.

1. **Assessment Alignment**
   — Compare and discuss final exams by grade level.
   — Compare and discuss other assessment tools: projects, writing pieces, tests (teacher made/ textbook provided).

2. **Curriculum Enhancement**
   — Discuss various teaching and learning strategies currently in use in our classes.
   — Display student products deriving from a variety of assignments and discuss learning demonstrated by them.
   — Share discoveries of new support materials for our units (DVDs, articles, etc.).

3. **Current Curriculum Review**
   — Discuss and evaluate current curriculum guide requirements: texts, titles, required writing, skills instruction, long-term projects, etc.
   — Gather revision suggestions in preparation for new adoption cycle.

4. **Department/Team Web Site**
   — Discuss possible content for our own Web site
   — Consider design, support, administration/oversight, use, etc.

Source: Linda Mihata, Lakeridge High School, English Department Chair. Used with permission.

FIGURE 5.4	Sample Professional Development Interest Self-Survey

Teacher Name: 　　　　　　　　　　　　　　　　　　　Department/Team:

Directions: Please complete this survey below by indicating the best possible answer to each question. We will use the results of this survey for the accreditation report and for planning next year's professional learning circles.

A. Considering where you are at this time, please identify your greatest need, in terms of specific professional development training:

B. Which of the following professional development training opportunities would you be most interested in and motivated to attend? (Please check all that apply.)

✓	
	Training in standards-based unit planning
	Training in standards-based grading
	Training in the use of the Critical Friends Process
	Training in how to promote higher-level thinking skills
	Training in how to promote teaming and collaboration skills by students in the classroom
	Training in how to use new technologies as learning tools for students
	Training in how to differentiate instruction in the classroom
	Training on learning styles of students and how to meet them
	Training in the effective use of formative assessment

C. Please respond to the statements below by checking the best response following the statement.	Yes	No	Not Sure
1. I have a clear understanding of the state standards that correspond to the content areas that I teach.			
2. I have a clear understanding of the difference between standards-based education and traditional teaching.			
3. I have a clear understanding of how to provide descriptive feedback to students.			
4. I have a clear understanding of how to design and use culminating assessments.			
5. I have a clear understanding of how to promote collaboration and teamwork among learners in the classroom.			
6. I have a clear understanding of student learning styles.			
7. I have a clear understanding of how to promote higher-level thinking skills among classroom learners.			
8. I have a clear understanding of the difference between formative and summative assessment.			
9. I have a clear understanding of how to develop quality standards-based unit plans.			
10. I have a clear understanding of how to use the Critical Friends Process to review student work.			
11. I have a clear understanding of how to effectively use formative assessment to increase student learning.			
12. I have a clear understanding of how to use formative assessment results to make changes in teaching.			
13. I have a clear understanding of how to differentiate instruction.			
Other comments related to professional development interests or needs:			

Source: Courtesy of D. Galera, Moanalua High School, Honolulu, Hawaii. Adapted with permission.

Moanalua's learning circles have included studies of interdisciplinary teaming, formative assessment, technology integration into classroom projects, common course assessments, and standards-based grading. These PLCs are ongoing learning opportunities where groups of teachers meet, fully investigate and study a strategy, implement it in their classes, and bring student work back to the group to share and analyze collaboratively.

Each learning circle cohort participates in a reflective activity at the end of the school year. This reflection takes the form of a professional conference with sessions run by the different learning circle members who present what they have learned and explain the difference it has made in their teaching and to their students' learning. The conference format brings all 130 certified faculty members together on a teacher professional day to publicly share and celebrate their learning. Each year, the school publishes its own professional journal, *Reflections: From Concepts to Classrooms,* to showcase individual and team efforts. Since 2000, teachers from other schools have been invited to attend this conference and view it as a model for ongoing professional development that works.

TOOLS
You Can Use

---→ Tool I (p. 147) is a template for a professional development interest self-survey.

There's a Dance for Everyone

Teams striving to reach the gold standard of professional learning must find a routine that resonates with their own circumstances and capacity and fits with their specific goals.

Simple Steps

If your team is just starting out, consider the following examples, which illustrate the variety of "beginning routines" available to you:

• The math teacher, who is a technology wizard, helps a small group of teachers gain expertise choosing and screening skill-based, interactive Web sites that will reinforce the curriculum and enhance student engagement with difficult math concepts.

• A reading teacher identifies reading strategies that cross curriculum lines and shares them with teachers on two interdisciplinary teams. The teachers go on to implement several of these strategies and track student successes throughout the semester.

• An English department reads the *Mosaic of Thought: Teaching Comprehension in a Reader's Workshop* by Keene and Zimmermann (1997) together and implements various year-long common strategies as their professional growth goal.

• The writing teacher shares the 6 + 1 writing traits rubrics, along with several teacher-generated rubrics, and the rest of the school adopts these rubrics as the basis for evaluating all students' written work. As a midyear check, a sample of student writing from various departments is blind scored, and the scores are used to generate further conversations and training to achieve the goal of writing across the curriculum.

• A mathematics teacher leader skilled in data analysis leads teams of teachers in a short inservice session focused on analyzing recent achievement test scores, then leads the group in a discussion of formative and summative assessment informed by *Classroom Assessment for Student Learning* by Stiggins, Chappius, Chappius, and Arter (2004).

• A science and math teacher team up to identify similar concepts that could form the basis for several units of cross-curricular study and bring the idea of developing these units to their departments, kicking off illuminating professional conversations.

More Advanced Steps

Perhaps your team has been together for a while. You have developed team relationships, and your initial efforts—sharing current teaching and learning practices—have been successful. Now, you're ready to combine a few of the beginning steps and take on a more complicated initiative. Consider these examples:

• A social studies teacher leader teams up with the art teacher, and they ask all students to create as a final project an abstract work to illustrate their understanding of the question "War: What is it good for?" As these two teachers collaborate, they videotape their lessons as a model of peer-to-peer observations. They videotape and share their lesson-planning conversations, their actual lessons, and post-lesson debriefing sessions as a model of peer-to-peer observations.

• A middle school team of teachers interested in increasing student engagement reads *Smart in the Middle Grades: Classrooms That Work for Bright Middle Schoolers* by Tomlinson and Doubet (2006). The team advances this initiative by asking a counselor and a talented and gifted teacher to provide assistance differentiating lessons. At the end of a set pilot period, team members share and analyze their lessons and student projects to see how effective they were in engaging students and challenging higher-level thinking.

• A team concerned about a high dropout rate among a subsection of its student population conducts an action research project on ways to address this issue by enhancing community connections. Using America's Promise materials and the 50 Cities Summit's connections to local businesses, the team creates an action plan and proceeds to launch a formal initiative before the school's parent community and the school board.

• The teacher leader of a team interested in peer-to-peer observations opens a meeting with a set of critical questions to consider, among them: *What exactly are peer-to-peer observations? Are we interested in observing one another's use of new strategies or tried-and-true ones? What training will we engage in prior to spending time in one another's classrooms? Will all team members be expected to participate?* As the group fleshes out questions and concerns, the teacher leader assures them that taking baby steps is perfectly fine: *Some of this is new to me, too. I'm used to an administrator observing me, so working with colleagues will feel different. I'll need to have help figuring this out. I think if someone could help me look objectively at what I'm doing as I practice teaching for transfer and literary analysis, that'd be a first step.* At the next meeting, the team watches several videotaped lessons together and uses the Peer-to-Peer Observation Framework (see Figure 5.5) to talk through how they will proceed. The teacher leader volunteers to be the first one observed.

FIGURE 5.5	A Peer-to-Peer Observation Framework

This framework structures the conversation between two teachers as they agree on the purpose of a one-to-one observation, prepares both teachers for the pre-observation conversation, sets the parameters for the observation, establishes the focus of the observation, and guides the reflective postconference that follows the observation session: Peer-to-peer observations provide an opportunity for a teacher to see a colleague teaching in his or her own classroom and to gather feedback that will help the person teaching analyze and improve his or her instructional or managerial practices.

Pre-observation: Two teachers meet and agree to work together as peers on a shared observation. They (1) set the day and time of the observation, (2) schedule the time and place to debrief the observation, (3) agree on the focus of the observation, (4) decide what data or information will be collected and shared, and (5) determine how data or information will be collected.

Observation: The observation will occur on the day and at the time arranged. The observing teacher will enter quietly, sit or move about as agreed, and collect data related to the agreed-on areas only. Although the observer will see other things of interest, to build trust in opening your classroom to another, the observation must stay within the agreed-on framework.

Postconference: Following the observation, the two teachers will debrief, taking time to reflect on what was seen and heard and considering how it might inform both their practices. Questions to consider include (1) How did it feel to be observed? How did it feel to observe? (2) What did the observing teacher learn? and (3) What might the observed teacher do differently next time?

Confidentiality: The observation notes will not be used in any evaluation, nor will they be used for any other purpose except as feedback to the individual being observed. Both teachers should be mindful not to share the details of the observation outside of agreed-on parameters. This is essential to building trust.

• A cross-curriculum group of content teachers explores interdisciplinary options together. They peruse individual unit plans submitted by team members and collaborate to identify common themes, concepts, and essential questions that cross the disciplines. As the group investigates what they have in common, they zero in on the essential questions that their students need to wrestle with in order to comprehend, analyze, or untangle the curriculum. These key ideas go on to guide the group's planning of interdisciplinary projects, use of class time, and assessment selection. Next on the docket? The development of a long-term course of interdisciplinary study so that their students' learning will be even more meaningful, relevant, and connected.

Seeking Outside Expertise

What if your team wants to explore an area that no one feels comfortable leading? One of the tenets of professional learning is that your team can grow in expertise together.

The number of professional learning resources available to teams is staggering. Selecting what your team needs is a matter of defining your areas of interest, examining materials to see how well they support your goals, and moving forward from there. Book studies are an excellent vehicle for exploring unfamiliar aspects of teaching and learning. Professional literature citing research and best practices is plentiful. There are also Web-based professional development options, DVDs with workbooks, online course options, and education-themed podcasts. All can help provide your team with a foundational understanding from which to proceed.

Talk with your principal and explore your school's professional association connections. Many of these associations provide reasonably priced resources and make them accessible regardless of your school's location. Also consider approaching the regional education laboratories, educational service districts, or the education departments at local colleges and universities.

After your team discusses the pros or cons of a new teaching practice, watches a DVD to learn about a new process, or attends an off-site seminar, the challenge is to connect this information to what is actually happening inside your classrooms. One way to begin making connections is to think back to your conversations about core values and the team purpose. What did the team decide its core values were? Focus on those that relate to how teachers teach and how students learn.

KAREN'S DILEMMA

Karen's team was ready to begin exploring formative assessment as a vehicle for professional growth. They had purchased several resources and designated time to work together each month. Karen was concerned because everyone else was a veteran teacher; when it came to classroom experience, she had the fewest years under her belt. She was not sure she could be effective leading the group's exploration of formative assessment, yet she was the designated leader. What if her teammates saw her as less than competent? The more Karen thought about this, the more uncomfortable she became. What should she do?

CONSIDER THESE KEY IDEAS AS YOU THINK ABOUT KAREN'S DILEMMA:

Relationships

- The beauty of being part of a team is that it encourages *shared* learning; the leader is not expected to be the expert in everything!
- Teacher leadership involves lots of modeling—and this includes modeling how to honestly express uncertainty, embrace risk taking, and ask others for advice and feedback.

Teaching and Learning

- Reflection, sharing best practices, and investigating new ways to address student learning needs should be at the top of every team's agenda.
- Celebrate progress related to team members learning and practicing new teaching strategies and methods in their classrooms.

OUR RESPONSE TO KAREN: THE FIRST STEP IS THE HARDEST

Yes, Karen is in an uncomfortable situation, but it's a common one for a teacher leader in collaborative learning environments, and as she gains experience with this role, she'll gain confidence. Any teacher leader facing this kind of dilemma is best served by being upfront with her teammates about her uncertainty. Remember that all team members are there to learn from one another; everyone has different skills, perspectives, and levels of expertise. What really counts is that the group discusses how to approach their new learning together and that each person takes responsibility for bringing information back to the group for discussion. It might be a book, an article, a DVD set—anything that will enrich the conversation.

As the team's leader, Karen's role is to facilitate conversations so that everyone—herself included—is learning and trying new strategies in the classroom and is sharing stories of their progress, setbacks, and clarified understanding. This is an interdependent professional learning community in action.

Leading the Dance

Every team's way of approaching professional learning will be different, because every team's members begin with different levels of skill and expertise. As the teacher leader, your role as academic facilitator and interpersonal coach means that sometimes you'll be called on to ask others to join this dance; sometimes you'll have the expertise necessary to be the dance instructor. Other teacher leaders may find themselves taking a more managerial role: finding the right music to correspond with the steps team members want to learn or finding the time for the team to actually practice the dance. Whatever the circumstance, the goal remains the same: taking the people you have and helping them embrace dancing as a way to come together. It is that combination of people and purpose that centers what your team is about.

What you must remember is that team efforts to improve practice through ongoing professional development and conversations about teaching and learning will flounder if they're put on a back burner or simply put off because real life or the team leader's personal discomfort gets in the way. Neither you nor the other members of your team will be able to master the steps if you don't all get up and practice them.

Fortunately, dance music can be intoxicating. When people hear it, they often begin tapping their toes to the beat, and, if the environment is welcoming, before they know it they've been enticed onto the dance

QUESTIONS
to Consider

- ⋯→ How does your group build professional expertise together?
- ⋯→ What resources or materials are available to you?
- ⋯→ What needs to change to make supporting adult professional growth a focal point of your team's work?

floor, regardless of their skill level. The energy generated by everyone giving their best effort supports team success and makes the effort fun.

According to Newmann and Wehlage (1995), "Schools need to have a clear, shared purpose for student learning, collaborative activity to achieve the purpose, and collective responsibility among teacher and students for student learning" (p. 51). We could not agree more. To paraphrase the well-known song by Lee Ann Womack, we hope you and your team will take that chance and join in this dance. Student success is in the balance.

ELISE'S DILEMMA

Competition runs high among Elise's department members. When she suggested pairing up to observe and give feedback to one another while they were trying out several new teaching strategies, she got panicked looks in return. One teacher asked if these observations would be part of the principal's evaluation. Another voiced strong objections to allowing another teacher into her classroom. Elise sensed that trust and collaboration were not the team's strong suit yet. She wondered where she should go from here.

CONSIDER THESE KEY IDEAS AS YOU THINK ABOUT ELISE'S DILEMMA:

Relationships

• There must be a clear expectation and commitment to work collaboratively.

• A team is made up of individuals, each with different skills, kinds of expertise, and comfort levels. Building community from a collection of individuals takes time, trust, and effort.

• Teacher leaders should validate the concerns and feelings of reluctant team members while gently moving the entire group forward.

- Teacher leaders who need help sorting through group dynamics should not be afraid to seek the advice of a colleague or another teacher leader.

Teaching and Learning

- It's a teacher leader's responsibility to initiate professional learning conversations focused on how the team will achieve agreed-on goals.
- Teaching and learning should always be at the center of what is done at school and in teams.
- Learning by doing is as important for adults as it is for students.

OUR RESPONSE TO ELISE: TAKING RISKS CAN MEAN BIG GAINS

This is a situation that calls for directness and honesty. The first thing Elise might do is assure the team that these observations will not be part of any evaluation, and they need have no concerns about this. Then, she ought to model the kind of response she'd like to see from the rest of the team by being the first to open her classroom doors to observation and focused, follow-up conversation about what she did and what observers saw.

Building trust is an incremental process. Teacher leaders facing this kind of dilemma should start with what *is* comfortable and expand. Perhaps Elise's group would be willing to have several lessons videotaped and viewed as part of establishing protocols for visiting one another's classrooms? Another option for her to consider would be to seek out professionally produced videos about teacher observation to give the group a better idea of what observers will need to focus on.

Great Resources on Strengthening Professional Practice

The following are all fine catalysts for team conversation and reflection.

• *Turning Points 2000: Educating Adolescents in the 21st Century* (Jackson et al., 2000) is a must-read for teachers exploring research-based best practices for engaging students in grades 5–10. Use the book study to identify strategies and practices your team wants to strengthen.

• *The Teaching Gap: Best Ideas from the World's Teachers for Improving Education in the Classroom* (Stigler & Hiebert, 1999) is a quick and easy read and worth sharing with team members as a way to move into a professional dialogue about the instruction actually going on in their classrooms. This professional reflection opens the door to further conversations about instructional improvement possibilities.

• *Mosaic of Thought: Teaching Comprehension in a Reader's Workshop* (Keene & Zimmermann, 1997) ought to be required reading to support the professional growth of anyone who teaches language arts from 4th grade through high school. You'll find this book makes a difference in how you think about and teach comprehension strategies to students, as it asks you to focus on metacognition. This is a sophisticated book, perfect for a departmental book study, and one you'll come back to time and time again as you hone your practice.

• *Failure Is Not an Option: Six Principles That Guide Student Achievement in High-Performing Schools* (Blankstein, 2006) takes on the issues at the heart of philosophical disagreements about who is responsible for learning. This book is particularly appropriate for a cross-curricular team ready to tackle grading practices. Digesting the points of the book can lead a team to revisit and revise instructional practices and assessments.

• *Fair Isn't Always Equal: Assessing and Grading in the Differentiated Classroom* (Wormeli, 2006) is another fabulous find for teachers and teams interested in differentiating instruction and serious about working through the complications that grading and assessment bring to this approach. For example, Chapter 8's look at grading practices that include effort, attendance, and behavior might set the stage for deep discussion. A special section of the book helps teacher leaders explore ways to support their colleagues with grading-related practice issues.

Some of the conversations this book starts may become uncomfortable, but the resulting insights and philosophical understandings may indeed change your practice.

DEAR DONNA

 FINDING THE FUN IN A FOCUS

DEAR DONNA.

This year our school teams were asked to work as learning communities on an academic goal for our team of students. My team decided to focus on writing across the curriculum and to score all student papers using a six-trait model. However, some other teams are pursuing service projects and team building as their goals. Kids are starting to compare, and they want off our team and on to a team that's doing something "fun"! I'm frustrated and a tad bitter. How should I deal with this?

AUDREY IN TACOMA

Dear Audrey,

Writing across the curriculum is a great team focus—one that will help your students make strong academic gains. However, it's true that a little fun is good for the spirit, so how about figuring out how to bring fun into this valuable initiative? For example, why not create a writing assignment that incorporates points of view and dialogue? Make it a newspaper or TV reporter project in which students (with teacher guidance) identify five or six places they can go in pairs or triads (with supervision and parent permission) to interview others and collect opinions, information, perspectives, and quotes. This is a field trip of sorts and could occur during a school day, if time and buses allow, because it's academically based but meets the "fun" definition of getting out of school and going to cool places: maybe a political rally, a teaching hospital, an animal shelter, a mall, or other places adults normally gather. The students' objective will be to take notes and incorporate the information gathered into an essay.

Also focus on celebrating accomplishments with special activities or even the occasional party. See if your team can find the balance between strong academic focus and celebrating work well done.

Donna

 DEALING WITH A NAY-SAYER

DEAR DONNA,

I love the work our team is doing on learning the new adopted curriculum. Unfortunately, one member of our team says he isn't ready to do the "new stuff" and he'll just wait until later. We all agreed to work together as a team and the team leader doesn't really address this problem, so I need some ideas on how to bring him along with the rest of us. He's a good teacher, and I think he will try things if we just can get him to work with us.

JENNIE FROM BISMARCK

Dear Jennie,

Lead by example! Your colleague may be a bit overwhelmed or underwhelmed with the new curriculum, so show him the possibilities. Set up some work sessions where everyone comes loaded with materials, ideas, and enthusiasm for developing a yearly calendar identifying the units you'll teach and the concepts and themes that will guide instruction. Then design lesson plans to be used and shared. See if everyone can meet in the reluctant teacher's classroom, and try to make these work sessions practical and useful. He'll see the light!

Donna

 ## PRESENTATION PANIC

DEAR DONNA,

I am the curriculum leader in social studies for our school. I received a memo from the district office asking me to prepare a 10-minute presentation for the school board, in which I am to report on teaching and learning strategies in my subject area as well as how social studies teachers in our school accommodate student learning needs. When I took on the role of our school's social studies curriculum leader, I certainly didn't expect to have to do something like this! How should I approach this task?

CHRIS FROM PORTLAND

Dear Chris,

It is true you signed on for a building-level position, but remember that being a teacher leader almost always includes "other duties as assigned." In this case, the school board sees you as part of a district leadership team representing your building. But I think you're more prepared than you think you are. You will be talking about two things you love: students and your subject area.

Connect the two. Explain to the school board how competent the social studies teachers are in your building and what you are all doing to ensure your students learn.

Donna

 ## GETTING THE PRINCIPAL'S SUPPORT

DEAR DONNA

As a result of my team deciding to participate in a new writing model called Writers' Workshop, we have developed a peer observation schedule where we visit one another's classrooms to observe and to present feedback on what we saw. The other teacher leaders in my school do not like this idea and have complained to the principal. The principal says we all do it or none of us do it. Any advice on how I can convince my principal that "one size doesn't fit all" and that we'd like to go ahead with an approach that fits us?

JACK FROM SAVANNAH

Dear Jack,

Peer observations can be scary for some. Perhaps your principal would be willing to have you and your team spend some time educating the staff on exactly what Writers' Workshop is and how you and your teammates incorporate data from peer observations to improve instructional opportunities for students. How about approaching the principal and team leaders with the idea that this is a pilot program and then arranging for constant information—including lesson plans, assessment tools, and so forth—to be presented to staff? Invite other teacher leaders, team members, and the principal into your classrooms to see what is happening there, and encourage other teams to participate or to develop similar goals for improving student achievement.

Donna

6

gauging progress

Most successful family road trips are not left to chance; they are undertaken only after serious calculations and thought. Once you and your family choose a destination, deliberations begin in earnest and become a story problem of mathematical proportion. A multitude of variables arise that must be considered. Calculations of all types figure in. How many days will you need to the destination? How many hours each day can the family sit together in the car? What kind of sightseeing might you do along the way? How many drivers might take turns at the wheel? It's only after all these planning decisions have been made that the trip can be plotted out in detail. Fortunately, the Automobile Association of America (AAA) stands ready to help with its online Trip-Tik Travel Planner. A few clicks of a mouse will generate a detailed road map from the point of trip origin to the final destination, noting mile posts, historic sites, sightseeing options, scenic overlooks, back roads, and major interstates.

This road map becomes both a guide and a feedback tool, helping your family reach your targeted destination happy and on schedule.

Targets Guide Team Success

At Lake Oswego Junior High School in Lake Oswego, Oregon, the planning and implementation of 8th grade English research projects are undertaken in much the same manner as you might plan a family road trip. To ensure that everyone, teachers and students, knows where they are going, all four teachers on the team begin by creating a final assessment checklist of the project criteria. Then they work backward, identifying major curricular standards embedded in the project, highlighting the various project requirements, setting due dates, laying out the grading rubric, outlining resources available to support key concepts, and trying to anticipate other pertinent details. All this information is shared with students at the very beginning of the project so that every student clearly understands the project's learning targets.

With these targets in place, the teachers can assist their students with the incremental steps needed to successfully and systematically achieve the learning objectives. The clearer a teacher is when defining learning targets in the classroom, the better students' chances are of learning what the teacher intends them to learn. And so, the students' final assessment checklist serves as both a guide that directs the journey and a feedback tool to let students and the teachers know how close each student is coming to hitting the learning target bull's-eye (Stiggins et al., 2004).

In this same fashion, team goals, set at the beginning of the year, become the targets teacher leaders and their teams use to guide the work they do. The clearer a team's learning goals and action plan, the more focused the collective work of the team becomes. During planning meetings for the team's teaching and learning initiative, take care to identify both the "end points" of the team's map and various check-in points along the way: where you will stop, assess progress, and make midcourse adjustments. Using feedback in this manner helps the team measure forward progress and keeps the team focused on their collective commitments. It's a feedback cycle that mirrors the family road trip, with the driver adjusting the route based on information from the navigator, who monitors both the AAA map and passengers' needs.

As Chen and Rybak (2004), experts in group processing, explain, "Assessment is an ongoing process within group work, not just a one-shot effort" (p. 352). Monitoring the group's work is essential to team success. It's your best chance of ensuring that all your team's hard work takes you and your students where you want to go.

Feedback and Learning

Educational writer and consultant Ron Brandt (1998) points out that everyone needs feedback to learn. Whether it is a newly formed team reading a book together to investigate a new teaching strategy for possible implementation or an established team collaboratively assessing student work, team members need to look at how they are working together, review their team goals, consider the strategies they are using to pursue these goals, reflect on these findings, and make informed adjustments. By taking these steps, teacher leaders and their teams will gain insights "that are instructive and instrumental to improving practice" (Barth, 2001, p. 128). They will also strengthen their learning community.

There are many ways teams can gather feedback regularly to ensure they are making progress toward their goals; some of these are formal, and others, less so. Something as simple as a quick thumbs-up, thumbs-sideways, or thumbs-down at the conclusion of a team meeting can gauge whether you're making progress or have stalled. Other informal feedback techniques include calling for a fist to five to indicate team members' satisfaction with a meeting's pace or focus and verbally going around the table and asking members what they plan to do prior to the next meeting to further work on the goal. You can also use written feedback, such as exit cards or quick writes, to assess the status of team members' expectations, pinpoint agreement, and solidify what will take place between one meeting and the next.

For a more formal assessment of a team's work, consider dedicating one team meeting to a midyear review activity. At this meeting, you might distribute copies of the team's goals and then ask each person to assess where he or she thinks the team is by jotting down answers to the following questions:

1. Is everyone still in agreement about the worthiness of the team's goals?

2. Does the team meet regularly and for the right purposes? Explain.

3. Is the time we spend discussing individual students balanced with a more general focus on teaching and learning?

4. Which of our common agreements are working, and which, if any, need additional focus?

5. What would make our meetings more fruitful?

6. What does the team need to do to further the team's adult-to-adult connections?

7. Reflect on your own role in moving our goals forward. Use the following codes to indicate where you are in relation to each goal: IP = in process, NA = needs attention, and NC/S = needs clarification and/or support.

There is tremendous value in asking team members to provide feedback not just on how well the team is functioning and progressing toward teaching and learning goals but also on how well they believe the team is being directed. For teacher leaders, regular self-reflection is helpful, but constructive feedback is critical. In our experience, most feedback team leaders receive from their team members affirms what is going well and underlines the teacher leader's confidence and competence in the leadership role.

Figure 6.1 provides a bank of survey items you might consider using as part of a midyear review to solicit feedback on your leadership and its effect on team operations. Find statements that parallel the work of your team and use them, adding any short-answer questions you might like to provide.

Perhaps you developed your leadership goals for the year in conference with the principal, using Tool B (see p. 140), introduced in

QUESTIONS *to Consider*

→ Does your team review and reflect on team goals throughout the year?

→ What markers are in place to check progress?

→ How do you collect feedback, and what do you do with it?

Chapter 2. In that case, you will want to ask for feedback that corresponds to progress you have made in those specific areas. If you have created personal or professional growth goals focused on the four leadership roles and responsibilities highlighted in Chapter 2 (interpersonal coach, academic facilitator, team manager, administration liaison), you might solicit feedback related to each of these quadrants (see Figure 6.2 for an example). When you distribute this kind of survey, encourage team members to respond honestly. As a teacher leader, you must reflect on the feedback you receive and use it to make adjustments that will improve your effectiveness as you work with the team.

There are also many good published surveys and checklists available to help a teacher leader and team analyze their work. We particularly recommend the ones offered in Robert J. Marzano's 2003 book, *What Works in Schools* (Chapter 17: "Take the Pulse of Your School")

TOOLS
You Can Use

···→ Tool J (p. 148) is a template for a team or team leader effectiveness survey.

···→ Tool K (p. 149) is a template for gathering team feedback on the four leadership responsibilities identified in Chapter 2.

FIGURE 6.1	Item Bank for a Leadership Feedback Survey

1. My team/department leader provides us with an agenda in a timely fashion.

2. Our reason for meeting is clear and understood by all.

3. We start and end our meetings on time.

4. Our work is centered on professional growth and meeting student needs.

5. Everyone has an opportunity to contribute during our meetings.

6. Our meetings are productive.

7. We discuss instructional strategies and best practices at our meetings.

8. We share successful lessons, activities, and assessments at our meetings.

9. Our team/department leader is approachable and responsive.

10. We develop goals for our team in a collaborative manner.

11. Everyone has a stake in our decision making.

12. Everyone has tasks and shares responsibilities.

13. We have respectful ways to handle conflict that are professional.

14. Our team/department leader recognizes individual contributions as well as team accomplishments.

and John Gabriel's 2005 book, *How to Thrive as a Teacher Leader* (the Appendix's Leadership and Climate Survey). Both books provide tools to help you assess team organization and communication, from goal setting to mediating conflicts and developing a positive environment to surveys that rate levels of satisfaction with other leadership roles. Be sure to share the essence of the feedback you receive (if not the specific set of responses gathered) after you have digested it, and always acknowledge your appreciation for team members' honest appraisal. If you add or revise goals based on this feedback, share those as well.

FIGURE 6.2	Sample Teacher Leadership Feedback Survey Response: The Four Areas of Responsibility

The four areas of responsibility listed below correspond to my roles as teacher leader. How well I serve you and how well we function as a team depend on my ability to carry out these roles. Please reflect on my work in each of these areas and give me some feedback in each area, being as candid as you can. Your feedback will help me reflect on my leadership, set goals, and refine my practice. Thanks in advance! Return these signed or unsigned to my mailbox by *June 12*.

Responsibility 1: Interpersonal Coach (communicating, listening, delegating, encouraging)	Responsibility 2: Academic Facilitator (selecting goals, creating learning opportunities, modeling)
I so appreciate your helping me figure out how to respond to Joey's dad's e-mail. You are a great mentor and friend.	Our goals seem so ambitious. For me, with three years of experience, it'd be better if I could take on just one or perhaps two. Plus, I need more help or training with the scoring we're all to do. Anyone else think that we took on too much? Can we talk about this?
Responsibility 3: Manager of the Team (organizing, developing systems and structures, carrying out team administration)	**Responsibility 4: Administrative Liaison** (advocating, representing, advising)
I like that we always know when and where we'll meet: good scheduling. However, it seems to me that we need to set ending times to our meetings. We seem to wander a lot, and then we're here trying to do business for two hours. That feels excessive, and I still have student work to correct.	You do a great job bringing the school leadership meeting updates to us. I feel like I know what the other teams here are doing and what we're up to as a school. Sometimes our faculty meetings are redundant! Any chance we could talk Mr. Lorain into giving us more August inservice time to do team things?

Any trip can have unexpected detours or roadblocks. Discussion of group feedback can help your team identify the ones you face and brainstorm how you might maneuver around them. Allow the conversation to pinpoint areas of the team's work that are strong and areas that need additional development. Identify needed resources, potential new activities, and corrective adjustments that will improve your collective ability to meet student needs. Of course, whenever you make an adjustment to a team goal or practice, it's a good idea to set a time to check in and review the effect this adjustment has had. With any assessment, or whenever you collect feedback, remember the goal is threefold: to make adjustments, to add an element of accountability to the team's efforts, and to share where the team is finding success.

KAREN'S AND RUBEN'S DILEMMA

By year's end, both Karen and Ruben felt good about the work they had done with their respective teams. Both could see that team members were collaborating more easily. They were sharing and acting in ways that showed new respect for each other. And Karen and Ruben both realized that they had grown in their role and now had a better sense of the tasks involved in leading a team.

Their respective principals asked each of them to provide written feedback, both a personal self-assessment and a collection of team feedback, about their year as leaders. This feedback, they were told, would be considered in setting future professional growth goals. Karen had outlined her goals earlier in the year, so she felt confident she could complete a self-reflection. Ruben was less confident. Neither of them had thought to ask their team members for feedback, but this struck them as a good idea. Ruben considered drafting several general feedback questions to pass out to his team. Karen wanted a more objective tool, as she was concerned the feedback from her team might be more critical. What should their next steps be?

USE THESE KEY IDEAS TO GUIDE YOUR THINKING ABOUT KAREN'S AND RUBEN'S DILEMMA:

Relationships

- Trust is built on honest and regular communication.
- Setting and sharing personal and professional leadership goals each year helps a teacher leader establish a team's direction.

Teaching and Learning

- Teams should regularly gather and use feedback data to assess and (if necessary) adjust professional learning goals.
- Team growth should be measured in terms of relationship building, members' engagement in learning, and this learning's effect on student achievement.

OUR RESPONSE TO KAREN AND RUBEN: ASK FOR FEEDBACK . . . AND USE IT

We would remind both these teacher leaders that asking for and gathering feedback about what's going well and what needs tweaking will help solidify the team. For example, Karen might consider using one of the objective instruments available online and from professional organizations. Ruben could ask open-ended questions about the team's progress toward their overall goals and about his leadership in each of the four major areas of responsibility. Either approach can generate valuable information.

Both should let the team members know they are receptive to their thoughts and will share all the feedback gathered with the rest of the group after they've had some time to digest it and consider how it might guide the team's work.

When the information comes in, Karen and Ruben should take a deep breath. Very likely they will learn some things they didn't know about themselves as leaders, which is as it should be. They, like all of us, will have areas for growth. We would also remind them that modeling this process of formatively assessing their work on the team paves the way for asking others on the team to do the same. This is how a team builds its capacity and forges tighter bonds.

Dealing with Detours and Breakdowns

Experienced road trippers know that sometimes the car breaks down, detours occur, major road construction disrupts the journey, and arguments flare up over who gets to sit by the window or where to stop for lunch. In schools, teacher leaders and teams face their own set of obstacles: The administration changes, new district initiatives are mandated and take precedence, budget cuts lead to less time for collaboration, a new member joins the team, or a team flounders and does not meet its goals.

It's when these events occur that the road map becomes an invaluable tool. A team's road map—its goals and action plan for achieving them—is constructed on the foundation of the team's common agreements and ground rules. Thus, the map is not only the metaphorical charting of a journey but also the vision of how this group of adults will work together collaboratively to create a culture where relationships are key to supporting improvements in teaching and learning.

An effective teacher leader understands that changes and challenges are inherent in schooling. Teacher leaders help their teams develop resilience by having a clear direction and purpose, by calling upon the team's shared vision, and by engaging team members' passion for teaching as a force to sustain the team's work. As Katzenbach and Smith (2003) note, it's by overcoming obstacles that a team "develops confidence in itself as a team, learns how to work more effectively together, and builds individual and collective skills in the process" (p. 167).

External Forces

Most administrators recognize and understand the complex factors needed to develop and sustain successful schools. Unfortunately, external factors and trends, like falling economics and budget reductions, can influence the operations and prevailing philosophies of schools. There are events and forces out of the principal's control that impact the work of teacher leaders and teams as they strive to help all students reach their potential. What does a teacher leader do when faced with these changes and competing challenges?

When times are uncertain or conditions change, effective teacher leaders know that to keep team morale high, they must fall back on the twin team fundamentals: (1) *who we are* (our relationships with one another) and (2) *what we are about* (teaching and learning to promote student success). Strong personal and professional relationships allow the team to look collectively at what has worked and adjust what the next steps might be. The teacher leader might need to redraw the road map with these external factors in mind. Sometimes that means redefining the team's or teacher's leadership goals. But the target remains the same: helping students reach their full potential.

Nancy Poliseno, a veteran teacher leader and team leader from Orange Middle School in Lewis Center, Ohio, has worked on two grade-level teams and under three principals with differing educational philosophies. She had this to say about avoiding potholes, navigating detours, and minimizing breakdowns:

> Keeping new teachers engaged and hopeful is indeed a very difficult task. Keeping "old" teachers engaged and hopeful is probably just as difficult. Trends in education seem to change quickly. I remind myself daily that I can sustain whatever change occurs as long as I take into account how it will affect my students and those with whom I work. Teacher leaders must be able to provide the stability to their team and staff when others are quick reactors to new initiatives. While it can be difficult to not "react" when something new is thrown in the already piled-high pile, it is important to sit back and reflect on issues at hand, reminding yourself and your team that the best teaching and education in the world is a combination of the "best of all practices, old and new." (personal correspondence, October 2008)

Sometimes changes and challenges present themselves as opportunities, which lead to other beneficial avenues for teacher leaders and their teams. Being flexible, being innovative, and viewing change and challenges as positives can make all the difference.

Internal Challenges

Not all changes and challenges are externally driven. Internal challenges do arise from time to time, and, if they're not addressed, they can sidetrack or block the work of the team. One of the most common challenges is tension within the team. Teacher leaders can often sense this, so surveying the team several times during the year, either informally or formally, is a reliable way to gauge team climate—and mediate any simmering conflicts before they affect team morale or function.

You might pose the following questions to your team and use the answers generated to jump-start deeper conversations:

- What is the definition of *team* that we are working toward?
- Are these expectations realistic or unrealistic?
- Do we define our team as an inclusive group and recognize that all of us have different approaches, strengths, and ways of operating?
- Is diverse thinking welcome?
- Can a team member be a teammate and at the same time maintain some degree of autonomy? What is that balance?
- Do we disagree without it leading team members to take sides and form cliques?
- How can we avoid meltdowns when tension surfaces?

The answers to these questions might reveal underlying conflict or misunderstanding. If this is the case, set aside a team meeting to discuss and resolve these relationship and professionalism issues.

Intervention Strategies

When tensions flare and disagreement turns divisive, the teacher leader has several options. Consider each of the following, along with its particular ramifications:

- Have a private conversation with one or more parties to discuss, verify, and resolve the problem.
- Take team time to acknowledge that a conflict may exist, and suggest a way to move around or through the issue.
- Bring in an outside facilitator to work with the team.
- Ask the principal for help.

Resources

Resources are available for the teacher leader needing help when the team is in trouble. Some teacher leaders feel confident tackling the issues on their own; others may want to bring in a trusted school counselor or another colleague to lead the entire team through a conflict resolution activity. One such exercise we can recommend, designed by Charlotte Roberts and Rick Ross and outlined in *The Fifth Discipline Fieldbook* (Senge et al., 1994), involves members anonymously submitting cards on which they "raise questions that never get raised" (p. 404) and an outside facilitator sorting these questions into categories and leading brainstorming sessions focused on how the team might respond. Remember, too, to seek support from building administrators and other teacher leaders. As important as it is to simply acknowledge a problem, taking the time to measure a conflict's potential impact and to seek outside assistance when necessary will be important to the long-term health of the team.

The End Goal

As a teacher leader, it is important to recognize the big picture and be mindful of all the elements, agendas, and circumstances that affect the day-to-day tactical work of teaching and teaming. Understand that all school improvement, whether undertaken through the team's work or addressed individually, is an extended endeavor. There will be clear beginnings and endings, and endings that are new beginnings. The end of the school year is a perfect time for engaging team members in reflection that prompts them to think about the year and summarize it in a way that makes sense personally. A team reflection exercise (see Figure 6.3) is an unusual and quirky way to do this.

FIGURE 6.3	Team Reflection Exercise

Purpose: To gather feedback from the group of adults who have worked together over a length of time that will shed light on the work accomplished and validate each person's contribution.

Process:

1. Using from six to eight words, participants write a "story" that tells how their work this year had affected them as a teacher and team member, then expand on that story through a paragraph-long narrative.

Examples: *We were challenged to think deeply, differently together.* (8 words)
Good friends, good conversations, what next? (6 words)
Loved it all, but so draining! (6 words)
So many initiatives; when can I just teach? (8 words)

2. Participants reread what they've written and identify ways that the team or team leader might wish to revise or restructure the work of the team in future.

3. Participants may share their stories if they wish, but the exercise is designed to be confidential and will be used for the sole purpose of helping the team work well together and move forward.

Because of the linear nature of the school calendar, begin each year with an orientation to the processes, structures, purpose, and vision that guide the team. This orientation should review past successes, identify what needs to be updated or changed, and set the stage for the future. Consider using artifacts of past team planning—such as team planning guides (see Tool E), team interest and resource maps (see Tool H), and professional development interest and feedback surveys (see Tool I) to help guide your next steps. Remember, everyone has a voice in these deliberations, so plan specific activities to bring new team members up-to-date. By working together, the past melds with the present.

Targeting the building of relationships and teamwide professional growth is the way to make students the beneficiaries of the team's work.

Celebrate throughout the process, use feedback to measure and guide progress, and remember that your job, as a teacher leader, is to "offer a balance between leadership that advances a school *program* by making it more suitable or rigorous, and leadership that moves *people* by strengthening their knowledge, skills, and commitment" (Little, 2000, p. 397). Intrepid teacher leaders create and consult a goal-centered map to guide this advancement, and they adjust the team's journey as needed so that everyone on and affected by the team—teachers and students alike—arrives at the desired destination.

ELISE'S DILEMMA

Earlier in the week, the principal came to ask Elise and her department team for feedback on his first year as their building leader. Elise knew her team had mixed feelings about the principal. He had not, for example, supported their efforts to hire substitutes so they could do peer observations, nor had he really understood their requests for more time to collaborate together during the school day for the purpose of assessing student work. Elise did feel the principal was beginning to understand and support their professional development. He was asking for feedback, which was certainly a positive thing. However, Elise was concerned that negative feedback from her team would blindside the principal and make it difficult for them to secure resources for next year. How could she approach the team with this caution in mind and still give her principal some constructive feedback?

 USE THESE KEY IDEAS TO GUIDE YOUR THINKING ABOUT ELISE'S DILEMMA:

Relationships

- The work in school depends on relationship building.
- Relationships are created over time and require a commitment to a common mission and ongoing engagement.

• Communication among team members and with the administration is a two-way responsibility critical for team success.

Teaching and Learning

• An important role of principals is to cultivate teacher leaders who will help improve the school's performance.

• Teaching and learning should center the work of the school and teacher teams.

OUR RESPONSE TO ELISE:
BE STRATEGIC, HONEST, AND RESPECTFUL

Building strong relations between the principal and the team and among team members is critical. These develop over time, based on communication, trust, respect, working together to move toward the school's vision, and an understanding of and sensitivity to one another's leadership style. With that in mind, Elise should let her team members know their feedback has been requested. She should help them think of areas where honest compliments are warranted. Then, together, they might identify areas that could be worth additional focus, phrasing it just like that: "worth additional focus." If teachers identify practices the principal might address, such as "develop a broader understanding of professional learning communities" or "identify areas for further shared leadership," these can generate great discussions.

If the team takes an antagonistic approach or attacks the principal for being unsupportive, defenses will go up and forward progress will be slowed. We would advise Elise and the rest of her team to be polite and professional. Clearly, if the year has been disastrous in terms of principal and style, they must communicate this feedback honestly, but a little diplomacy, respect, and data can go a long way in bridging understanding. They might begin by encouraging the principal to attend team meetings and inservice sessions to observe and experience the team's attention to teaching and learning and see in person how this has increased student success.

Effective leadership comes in many styles; working for the success of all students is the long-term goal, and when that is supported, you have time and opportunity to shape how that comes about.

Great Resources to Support Gauging Progress

• As you know by now, we highly recommend *The Team Handbook* (Scholtes et al., 2003), particularly for those times when you find your team in trouble. Take a look especially at Chapter 6's discussion of constructive feedback, Chapter 13's Meeting Skills Checklist (Exercise #2), and Chapter 7's look at common problems and solution strategies. If you purchase this book, you can retrieve downloadable worksheets, matrices, and checklists from www.orielmc.com.

• Chapter 8 of *The Wisdom of Teams* (Katzenbach & Smith, 2003) presents six clear strategies (ranging from refocusing on performance goals to reformatting the team) for surmounting obstacles and getting a team unstuck.

• *Assessment for Learning: An Action Guide for School Leaders* (Chappuis, Stiggins, Arter, & Chappuis, 2005), from the Assessment Training Institute, is a teacher-friendly book and DVD from Rick Stiggins and his colleagues. It's a good choice for teams looking to examine their practices and strengthen classroom formative assessment techniques. You'll also find activities that will help teachers translate learning targets into student-friendly language, a student survey about assessments, excellent advice on using feedback to set goals, grading scenarios, and tips for connecting assessment to reporting.

DEAR DONNA

 A FRIEND WHO BENDS THE RULES

DEAR DONNA,

I am a team leader for a group of teachers in our elementary school. My very best friend is a 5th grade teacher and an excellent one. She loves the students and supports what we do as a team, but she seems to feel she can get away with things others cannot because she is my best friend. She takes liberties, without my knowledge or approval, and it is causing a great deal of tension on the team. I've hinted we need to be fair and let everyone do things, but that hasn't helped. Should I leave it alone, or is there some way to resolve this so she knows others want to be part of the team as well? I value her friendship, but this can't continue. What can I do?

GAIL IN OLYMPIA

Dear Gail,

It won't be easy, but you really must address the issue with your friend—first in private. Explain to her your personal goals and philosophy for leading the team, and give her specific examples of how you attempt to carry them out. Remind her of the difference between leadership carried out by one or two and the shared leadership you strive for in your team. Do make sure she feels valued as part of the team, and then carefully steer the team in a direction where all are treated equally.

Taking the time to solicit informal feedback from all team members about how the team is operating and to review the team's common agreements on a regular basis can bring these kinds of issues to everyone's attention in a way that isn't pointing a finger or assigning blame. This might be something for you to consider as your next step as well.

If your friend is still taking liberties at this point, she may need to be reassigned to another team. But my guess is she will see what's happening and be grateful that you gave her this feedback.

Donna

 TAKING IT PERSONALLY

DEAR DONNA,

This year the principal selected me to replace a veteran teacher who had been in our school leadership structure for years. Now the teacher I replaced talks behind my back, questions my ability to lead, and basically tries to sabotage everything I try to do. What do you suggest I do?

ALEX IN CHICAGO

Dear Alex,

Schools are social institutions; sometimes relationships sour, and it feels so personal when that happens. In this case, it is necessary to approach the former teacher leader in a private setting and state clearly that you have heard the comments made about you and you are interested in finding a way to move past this so the two of you can work together in a positive way. Using "I" messages to share your feelings and concerns can be an effective way for you to reestablish communication with the teacher leader you replaced. Here are three you might try:

1. *When I hear the comments you have made about me, I feel devalued and it makes me angry. Perhaps with the change in leadership you just experienced, you may be feeling the same way....*

2. *I hope we can find common ground and work together in positive and constructive ways. I value your leadership experience and teaching expertise, and I will always listen to your interests, ideas, and concerns.*

3. *I am new at leadership, and I know I will make mistakes. I hope I can come to you for advice and for support. I feel it is important for us to work together as a team, and I hope you will help me as I begin this new phase in my educational experience.*

If this doesn't resolve the issue, or if your approaches are rebuffed, take the information to the principal and ask for assistance. When you do, try to resist speaking ill of the former leader. Better by far to focus on ways you might forge a new relationship. Perhaps the former leader is embarrassed, hurt, and grieving. You can be the one to reach out to begin the healing.

Donna

SEEKING ANSWERS ... OR AN OUT

DEAR DONNA,

Last week my principal called me into her office and told me she was replacing me as a teacher leader. She didn't give me a reason, and I feel so devalued and so unsupported. I don't think I can ever work with this principal again. I am even considering transferring to another building. What do you think?

KATHY IN HOUSTON

Dear Kathy,

What you experienced was hurtful, without a doubt. You need some answers. I would suggest you request a meeting with the principal in your classroom or in a neutral place—not her office. Give her a list of the questions you want answered ahead of time so she can prepare for the meeting. The answers might not be what you expect or what you want to hear, but finding some closure to this is really important.

At that point, yes, you will have a decision to make. If you cannot find resolution to this situation, transferring to another building might be an option for you. You do need to move ahead with your personal and professional life, so seek clarity and strive for balance within the circumstances.

Donna

conclusion

**Build structures and systems,
but leave the door open to serendipity.**

—Garnetta Wilker

As a library-media specialist and curriculum expert, Garnetta Wilker understands the critical interplay between relationships and teaching that engages students in learning. In her role, she collaborates with teachers and teacher teams to use curriculum to design learning experiences that allow students to open doors and soar. As a teacher leader, she realizes the importance of having a framework to guide team endeavors while also allowing enough flexibility to embrace possibilities and the unexpected opportunities that come along. The opening words of this section are her leadership mantra.

Build Structures and Systems

There are as many variations of teacher leaders as there are teams and schools. Although there is no single approach that guarantees success, what is clear is that there are skills, processes, and structures that can help teacher leaders be effective and positively influence the work that occurs in their teams.

A growing body of literature confirms that the two ingredients critical in any successful recipe for leading teams of teachers are a *focus on positive, productive relationships* and *attention to teaching and learning* (Fullan, 2001; Jackson et al., 2000; Marzano, 2003). Achieving the interdependence between relationships and professional practice, between people and purpose, is key. In this book, we provide our perspective on what this entails and how to approach these aspects of the teacher-leader role. Although teacher leadership involves more than working one's way through a list of the role's responsibilities, for a beginning teacher leader, a simple checklist can be helpful as an overview and a reminder of the role's "other duties as assigned."

Throughout this book, we've used metaphors to introduce the ideas, skills, and purpose behind teacher leadership and to offer entry points to the work of building leadership capacity. We've talked about

TOOLS
You Can Use

Tool L (p. 150) is a checklist for a teacher leader, covering both readiness for the role and the role's responsibilities.

• The school as a mosaic that comprises the contributions of many individuals.

• Shared leadership as an exhilarating and sometimes scary river rafting trip, during which individuals build and grow interdependence through collaboration, collegiality, community, cooperation, and communication.

• The teacher who leads a team as a rubber band: flexible, elastic, and focused on not only joining individuals into a group but also helping the group find a collective identity and purpose.

• Laying the foundation for the teamwork process by constructing a framework and installing the nuts, bolts, and rivets that will help the group operate efficiently and effectively.

• Forging links that will bind a team together as a community with common beliefs, values, and goals.

• Mastering the dance of continuous teaching-and-learning improvement by examining current instructional practices and identifying and implementing new practices, techniques, and tools that will increase student success.

• Embarking on the "road trip," a journey that includes pursuing team goals, agreeing on the destination, stopping along the way to check progress, and finding alternate routes as necessary.

We hope these metaphors will help you, as a teacher leader, make sense of the complicated priorities, underlying assumptions, and varying tasks necessary to mold a group of peers into an effective, productive team.

Effective teacher leaders understand that the interdependence between relationships (people) and a focus on teaching and learning (purpose) is key to the teacher leadership recipe, and they are able to fold these together to make a complicated recipe seem simple. And just as individual cooks will vary a recipe to satisfy personal tastes or suit particular occasions, every teacher leader can be expected to add his or her signature to this recipe by blending in past experiences, imagination, personal philosophy, attitude, temperament, and talents.

So as you move forward, follow any recipe that creates structures and systems for adults to collaborate with other adults; add a measured amount of purpose; throw in a pinch of individual leadership style; and then stir, mix, blend, and fold together gently. Teams, like perfectly prepared meals, take patience, care, and attention.

... But Leave the Door Open to Serendipity

Effective teacher leaders know, too, that they and their teams will face unpredictable events and plenty of surprises. Recognize these moments, and embrace them as opportunities. These are the unexpected spices and flavors that make life in a school, in a classroom, and on a team fresh and original. This is where magic can happen. It has for Garnetta and her teams, and we hope you approach your work as teacher leader in much the same way.

You have our recipe. We're excited to see what you will make of it.

DEAR DONNA

 MAKING IT WORK

DEAR DONNA,

For this coming school year, my district has assigned me to help the principal prepare for the opening of our newest high school. Because I am an experienced teacher, my primary responsibilities will be to design a model for shared leadership, work on inservice training options, and pull together the school's curriculum offerings. Once this basic work is complete, the staff will be chosen, leadership positions will be filled, and I will return to my previous assignment. I am looking for perspectives on how to proceed, and I would appreciate hearing what you have to say.

CHRISTINE IN BOTHELL

Dear Christine,

Working to design a shared leadership model in which the academic success of all students is valued and celebrated is exciting and important work.

Begin by setting an overarching goal to guide the work you will do and the decisions you will make. If such a goal has not yet been set, allow me to suggest a possibility: *Our school strives to build strong, supportive relationships among staff, students, parents, and community while valuing academic success for all students.*

With a goal like this in place, your work will be the road map for building supportive relationships and for developing a strong, flexible academic program. Letting everyone know upfront what the target goal is can promote conversations with your colleagues about how you'll go about creating the leadership, curriculum, and necessary support services to meet that goal.

It's important to be clear about your leadership model. Be sure you can articulate what shared leadership is and how it will work in this school. Some questions for you to consider include *What are the criteria for selecting teacher leaders? How do teachers apply, and to whom? Who makes decisions about filling the leadership positions? What is a teacher leader's term of service? How is leadership shared? What does the administrator do? What do teachers do? How is information communicated to staff?*

Problems with leadership develop when the work of leaders is not openly shared with staff. Make sure you develop a strong communication system; communication must be a two-way responsibility from the get-go! You might also consider developing a problem-solving process in which staff who have issues can bring them to the leadership team or to the administrative team and be assured of a quick and fair resolution.

When developing a curriculum for the new school, your premise must be that the academic offerings need to work for *all* students, of all ability levels. You will work within the content constraints of your state and district, so some of your work can focus on how to adapt these courses to the academic needs of all students. Even teachers of AP or IB classes will still need help with strategies, processes, and procedures for differentiating instruction. Perhaps your inservice programs for the first year could be in this area.

When you finish the work of creating a shared leadership model, and when the academic portion of your work is complete, turn your attention to developing a framework for celebrations: a way to recognize the interests and efforts of faculty, staff, administration, and students. Why celebrations? Celebrations bring a school community together and provide strength for future endeavors.

This is your opportunity to start traditions that will ground the school for years to come. Perhaps the school leadership team might be interested in developing a schoolwide student incentive program? As academic teams are formed, and as they begin their work with students, the leadership team can recognize and support the efforts of individual teams in further developing ideas for team celebrations.

When goals are met, when success is honored, and when relationships are valued, schools coalesce into communities that work academically and socially and where everyone thrives. There is so much more to be said, but the best advice I can give to you is to always remember to keep your target goal in mind.

Donna

a teacher leader's toolkit

Interactive versions of these tools are available for download in a password-protected PDF format from the ASCD Web site (www.ascd.org). Follow the Publications link to the Books page, select "Browse by Title," and then select this book's title. To access the PDFs, enter the case-sensitive password *ASCD109075*.

Tool A | Self-Reflection Exercise: You as the Teacher Leader

Check those items that reflect your preferences, interpreting each descriptor as you understand it.

Type of Leader

____ inexperienced

____ experienced

____ traditional

____ visionary

____ shared

____ collaborative

Characteristics as Leader

____ creative thinker

____ risk taker

____ problem solver

____ good manager

____ analyzer

____ doer

____ thinker

____ decision maker

____ coordinator

____ pleaser

____ consensus builder

____ sharer

____ collaborator

Preferred Working Style

____ independently

____ in a group

____ depends on the task

Preferred Team Structure

____ traditional

____ curriculum based

____ task or initiative based

____ professional learning community (PLC)

Look at where you placed your check marks. What kind of leader do you seem to be?

Now, check all of the *Group Member Characteristics* that apply to you.

I…

_____ am quick to praise others

_____ like to consider all ideas before making a decision

_____ believe my ideas are sound and usually the best

_____ bring dissenting voices together to find common ground

_____ embrace laughter and humor as part of group work

_____ find solutions to conflicts

_____ compromise easily

_____ draw others into the group

_____ like to set goals and standards

_____ like to set agendas and conduct meetings

_____ use processes and procedures in meetings

_____ keep detailed notes or records

_____ share my options and feedback readily

_____ enjoy sharing data or important information

_____ have the ability to summarize or clarify main points

_____ ask questions for clarification or direction

_____ participate in discussions

_____ prefer to listen rather than talk

_____ expect the designated leader to lead

_____ prefer to work from an agenda

_____ express discontent during meetings

_____ express discontent to other group members after a meeting

_____ accept group decisions

_____ feel positive in thought and action

_____ enjoy working with others

_____ prefer to work alone

_____ tend to feel isolated in a group situation

_____ value everyone's point of view as valid and legitimate

_____ feel confident about my abilities

_____ tend to dominate or control conversations

_____ stick to my own point of view

Finally, take a look at the whole picture. Having completed this self-reflection exercise, how would you describe yourself as a leader and as a member of a group? Are there any barriers or obstacles that you might address to make yourself a more effective team leader? How could you go about this? To help you get started, read and reflect on "Improving Relationships Within the School-house," a provocative article by Roland Barth published in the March 2006 issue of *Educational Leadership*.

Tool B | Goal Development Template for Teacher Leaders

Name: _____

School: _____

Current Position: _____

Leadership Assignment: _____

Date: _____

Annual Review Date: _____

Supervisor: _____

Goal Development Guidelines:

Please draft two leadership goals for the year; be sure to identify ways these goals can be measured, and outline the resources or support you will need to meet them. Bring these with you to a meeting with your supervising administrator. You will engage in a conversation to finalize these goals.

Goal 1a: Professional Leadership Goal
(such as increase peer support options within the team by _____, *develop protocols for* _____ *)*

1b: Evaluation Method:

1c: Resources/Support:
(such as workshop, university course, training, read & conference)

Goal #2a: Personal Leadership Growth Goal
(such as skill development, increase use of processes, organizational focus)

2b: Evaluation Method:

2c: Resources/Support

Tool C | Team Meeting Agenda Template

Meeting Date: _____

Meeting Place: _____

Materials Needed: _____

Agenda Item	Action (e.g., Discuss/Develop/Accept/Modify....)	Time

Carry-In/Last-Minute Agenda Items:

Updates/Information to Share:

Tool D | Team Meeting Minutes Template

Date: _____

Attendance: _____

Absent/Who Will Share Info? _____

_____

Agenda Item: Presented by:

Discussion:

☐ Action   By Whom: When:

☐ Action   By Whom: When:

Agenda Item: Presented by:

Discussion:

☐ Action   By Whom: When:

☐ Action   By Whom: When:

Agenda Item: Presented by:

Discussion:

☐ Action   By Whom: When:

☐ Action   By Whom: When:

Tool E | Team Planning Guide Template

Members: _____

Date: _____

Big ideas we want to explore:

Our strengths:

Areas we need/want to build:

Resources that would help us address these areas (e.g., money, materials, time exchange, visitations, business connections, Web sites, online training):

Local sources of expertise to help us with our targeted areas:

What we might offer in exchange (e.g., bartering expertise, services, materials, products):

Remember: The idea is to build networks with others in the school, the district, and neighboring districts, nearby colleges and universities, or professional organizations so that a lack of financial resources doesn't impede progress!

Tool F | Team Improvement Plan Template

Team: _____   Teacher Leader: _____

Date: _____

School Goal: _____

Team Goal: _____

Intended Outcome	Planned Activities	Target Dates	Individuals Involved	Resources/ Expenses

Tool G | Tally the Talk Grid Template

Team: _____   Date: _____   Completed by: _____

Teacher	Social/ Collegial Talk	Personal Talk	Organizational Talk	General Student Talk	Learning- Focused Student Talk	Curriculum Instruction Assessment Talk	Comments

Other Notes/Comments:

Tool H | Team Resource and Interest Map Template

What We Do Well: Effective Strategies and Methods

What We Read Professionally: Education-Focused Reading over the Past 9 Months

What We Would Like to Investigate: Strategies and Methods, Books, Research

Actions We Might Take

Tool I | Professional Development Interest and Feedback Survey Template

Teacher Name: _____   Department/Team: _____

Survey Directions:

A. Considering where you are at this time, please identify your greatest need, in terms of specific professional development training: _____

B. Which of the following professional development training opportunities would you be most interested in and motivated to attend? (Please check all that apply.)

✓	

C. Please respond to the statements below by checking the best response following the statement.

	Yes	No	Not Sure

Other comments:

Tool J | Team/Team Leader Effectiveness Survey Template

Team: _____

Date: _____

For each statement listed below, check the box that reflects your thinking and experience.

Statement	Needs Work	Somewhat Effective	Effective	Very Effective

General Comments:

Suggestions for Improvement:

Tool K | Teacher Leadership Feedback Survey Template: The Four Areas of Responsibility

The four areas of responsibility listed below correspond to my roles as teacher leader. How well I serve you and how well we function as a team depend on my ability to carry out these roles. Please reflect on my work in each of these areas and give me some feedback in each area, being as candid as you can. Your feedback will help me reflect on my leadership, set goals, and refine my practice. Thanks in advance! Return these signed or unsigned to my mailbox by _____.

Responsibility 1: Interpersonal Coach (communicating, listening, delegating, encouraging)	**Responsibility 2: Academic Facilitator** (selecting goals, creating learning opportunities, modeling)
Responsibility 3: Manager of the Team (organizing, developing systems and structures, carrying out team administration)	**Responsibility 4: Administrative Liaison** (advocating, representing, advising)

Tool L | A Teacher Leader's Checklist

Readiness Assessment

☐ I have a leadership position in mind: _____ .

☐ I have assessed my own strengths/areas for growth and compared them to the position.

☐ I understand the role and responsibilities of the leadership position.

☐ I have expressed my interest in this position to the administration.

☐ I have _____ years of experience teaching _____ (subject).

☐ I have taken the lead on other activities, including _____

_____ .

To-Do List

☐ Share leadership/team vision with team members.

☐ Draft a long-term plan/goals that align with the school's mission.

☐ Ask team members for input.

☐ Develop common agreements with the team.

☐ Set meeting times, procedures, and structure.

☐ Develop a team communication plan.

☐ Organize tasks.

☐ Strengthen relationships with team members and the administration.

☐ Follow up on assigned tasks.

☐ Facilitate team development.

☐ Identify possible traditions and discuss with the team.

☐ Monitor morale.

☐ Ask for team feedback; use this to adjust goals and direction.

references and resources

Ancess, J. (2008, May). Small alone is not enough. *Educational Leadership, 65*(8), 48–53.

Arnold, J., & Stevenson, C. (1998). *Teachers teaming handbook: A middle level planning guide.* New York: Harcourt Brace.

Barth, R. S. (2001). *Learning by heart.* San Francisco: Jossey-Bass.

Barth, R. S. (2006, March). Improving relationships within the schoolhouse. *Educational Leadership, 63*(3), 9–13.

Blankstein, A. M. (2006). *Failure is not an option: Six principles that guide student achievement in high-performing schools.* Thousand Oaks, CA: Corwin.

Brandt, R. (1998). *Powerful learning.* Alexandria, VA: ASCD.

Burgess, J. (2007, October). 50 things successful leaders do: Giving VOICE to what works. *Middle Ground, 11*(2), 27.

Burgess, J. (2008). *A smart start for professional development: From sticky notes to dragon boats, 20 slightly off-kilter activities for middle schools.* Westerville, OH: National Middle School Association.

Burke, J. (2000). *Reading reminders: Tools, tips, and techniques.* Portsmouth, NH: Boynton/Cook Publishers.

Chappuis, S., Stiggins, R., Arter, J., & Chappuis, J. (2005). *Assessment for learning: An action guide for school leaders* (2nd ed.). Portland, OR: Assessment Training Institute.

Chen, M., & Rybak, C. J. (2004). *Group leadership skills: Interpersonal process in group counseling and therapy.* Belmont, CA: Brooks/Cole.

Collins, J. (2001). *Good to great: Why some companies make the leap ... and others don't.* New York: HarperBusiness.

Danielson, C. (2007, September). The many faces of leadership. *Educational Leadership, 65*(1), 14–19.

Deitel, B. (2000, February). Team work: Teaching partnerships pass the test. *Middle Ground, 3*(4), 10–14.

Devaney, K. (1987). *The lead teacher: Ways to begin.* New York: Carnegie Forum on Education and the Economy.

Donaldson, G. G., Jr. (2006). *Cultivating leadership in schools: Connecting people, purpose, and practice.* New York: Teachers College Press.

DuFour, R. (2004, May). What is a "professional learning community"? *Educational Leadership, 61*(8), 6–11.

DuFour, R., & Eaker, R. (1998). *Professional learning communities at work: Best practices for enhancing student achievement.* Bloomington, IN: National Education Service.

Dutton, J. (2007, September/October). *Energize your workplace: Executive summary.* EDge: A Phi Delta Kappan Publication. San Francisco: Jossey-Bass.

Fullan, M. (2001). *Leading in a culture of change.* San Francisco: Jossey-Bass.

Gabriel, J. G. (2005). *How to thrive as a teacher leader.* Alexandria, VA: ASCD.

Goleman, D., Boyatzis, R., & McKee, A. (2002). *Primal leadership: Learning to lead with emotional intelligence.* Boston: Harvard Business School Press.

Graham, B. I., & Fahey, K. (1999, March). School leaders look at student work. *Educational Leadership, 56*(6), 25–27.

Greenfield, W. (2005). Leading the teacher work group. In L. W. Hughes (Ed.), *Current issues in school leadership* (pp. 245–264). Mahwah, NJ: Erlbaum Associates.

Hargreaves, A., & Shirley, D. (2008, October). The fourth way of change. *Educational Leadership, 66*(2), 56–61.

Harrison, C., & Killion, J. (2007, September). Ten roles for teacher leaders. *Educational Leadership, 65*(1), 74–77.

Harvey, S., & Goudvis, A. (2000). *Strategies that work.* York, MA: Stenhouse.

Heifetz, R. A., & Linsky, M. (2002). *Leadership on the line: Staying alive through the dangers of leading.* Boston: Harvard Business School Press.

Jackson, A., Davis, G., Aheel, M., & Bordonaro, A. (2000). *Turning points 2000: Educating adolescents in the 21st century.* The Carnegie Council on Adolescent Development. New York: Teachers College Press.

Katzenbach, J. R., & Smith, D. K. (2003). *The wisdom of teams: Creating the high-performance organization.* New York: HarperCollins.

Keene, E. O., & Zimmermann, S. (1997). *Mosaic of thought: Teaching comprehension in a reader's workshop.* Portsmouth, NH: Heineman.

Liebermann, A., Saxl, E. R., & Miles, M. B. (2000). Teacher leadership: Ideology and practice. In M. Fullan (Ed.), *The Jossey-Bass reader on educational leadership* (pp. 348–365). San Francisco: Jossey-Bass.

Lipsitz, J., & Felner, R. (1997). What works in middle grades schools reform. *Phi Delta Kappan 78*(7), 517–556.

Little, J. W. (1997). Teachers' professional development in a climate of education reform. In *The challenge of school change* (pp. 137–178). Arlington Heights, IL: IRI Skylight Training & Publication.

Little, J. W. (2000). Assessing the prospects for teacher leadership. In M. Fullan, (Ed.), *The Jossey-Bass reader on educational leadership* (pp. 390–418). San Francisco: Jossey-Bass.

Loucks-Horsley, S. (1996). *Principles of effective professional development for mathematics and science education: A synthesis of standards.* Madison, WI: National Institute for Science Education. (ERIC document reproduction service No. ED 409 201).

Marzano, R. J. (2003). *What works in schools: Translating research into action.* Alexandria, VA: ASCD.

McTighe, J., & Wiggins, G. (2004). *Understanding by design professional development workbook.* Alexandria, VA: ASCD.

Miller, D. (2002). *Reading with meaning: Teaching comprehension in the primary grades.* Portland, MA: Stenhouse Publications.

National Association of Secondary School Principals. (2004). *Breaking ranks and breaking ranks II: Strategies for leading high school reform.* Reston, VA: Author. Available: www.principals.org

National Association of Secondary School Principals. (2006). *Breaking ranks in the middle.* Reston, VA: Author. Available: www.principals.org

National Center for Essential Schools Northwest. (n.d.). *Critical friends groups.* Available: www.cesnorthwest.org/cfg.php

National Middle School Association. (2003). *This we believe: Successful schools for young adolescents.* Westerville, OH: Author.

National Middle School Association. (2005). *This we believe in action: Implementing successful middle level schools.* Westerville, OH: Author.

National Staff Development Council. (2008). *Learning communities.* Available: www.nsdc.org/standards/learningcommunities.cfm

Newmann, F. M., & Wehlage, G. G. (1995). *Successful school restructuring: A report to the public and educators.* Madison, WI: Center on Organization and Restructuring of Schools, Wisconsin Center for Educational Research.

Quint, J. (2008, May). Lessons from leading models. *Educational Leadership, 65*(8), 64–68.

Scholtes, P. R., Joiner, B. L., & Streibel, B. J. (2003). *The team handbook: How to use teams to improve quality* (3rd ed.). Madison, WI: Oriel, Inc.

Schurr, S., & Lounsbury, J. (2001). *Professional development kit #3: Revitalizing teams to improve student learning.* Westerville, OH: National Middle School Association.

Senge, P. M. (1990). *The fifth discipline: The art and practice of the learning organization.* New York: Doubleday/Currency.

Senge, P. M., Kleiner, A., Roberts, C., Ross, R. B., & Smith, B. J. (1994). *The fifth discipline fieldbook: Tools and strategies for building a learning organization.* New York: Doubleday/Currency.

Singleton, G. E., & Linton, C. (2005). *Courageous conversations about race: A field guide for achieving equity in schools.* Thousand Oaks, CA: Corwin.

Stiggins, R., Chappius, S., Chappius, J., & Arter, J. A. (2004). *Classroom assessment for student learning: Doing it right, doing it well.* Portland, OR: Assessment Training Institute.

Stigler, J. W., & Hiebert, J. (1999). *The teaching gap: Best ideas from the world's teachers for improving education in the classroom.* New York: Free Press.

Tomlinson, C. A., & Doubet, K. (2006). *Smart in the middle grades: Classrooms that work for bright middle schoolers.* Westerville, OH: National Middle School Association.

Ullock, K. H. (2004). *The importance of teaming* [DVD]. Westerville, OH: National Middle School Association.

U.S. Department of Education, Office of Educational Research and Improvement. (2001). *Creating high performing and equitable schools.* The High Performing Learning Community Project. Emeryville, CA: RPP International in collaboration with California Tomorrow and Bay CBS.

Waters, T., & Grubb, S. (2004). *Leading schools: Distinguishing the essential from the important.* Aurora, CO: Mid-continent Research for Education and Learning.

Wheatley, M. (2000). Good-bye, command and control. In M. Fullan (Ed.), *The Jossey-Bass reader on educational leadership* (pp. 339–347). San Francisco: Jossey-Bass.

Wiggins, G., & McTighe, J. (2005). *Understanding by design* (2nd ed.). Alexandria, VA. ASCD.

Wormeli, R. (2006). *Fair isn't always equal: Assessing and grading in the differentiated classroom.* York, MA: Stenhouse.

Index

The letter *f* following a page number denotes a figure.

about the authors

Jan Burgess spent 24 years in school administration, primarily as an elementary and middle school principal, following eight years as a teacher and counselor. Her work with teacher leaders over those years formed the crux of her understanding of shared leadership as the model for creating and maintaining outstanding learning environments for students.

Jan earned her bachelor's degree in Elementary Education from Lewis and Clark College, Portland, Oregon, and a master's degree in Guidance and Counseling from Portland State University. She has credentials in administration and educational leadership.

An author, Jan has published numerous articles in educational journals and the book *A Smart Start for Professional Development: From Sticky Notes to Dragon Boats, 20 Slightly Off-Kilter Activities for Middle Schools*.

Jan can be reached at 6120 SW Chestnut Avenue, Beaverton, Oregon 97005, or at jbb2@comcast.net.

Donna Bates has more than 30 years of elementary- and middle-level teaching experience. She has served as an elementary team leader, a middle-level curriculum leader, and a teacher association president. She has also been a member and leader of a number of district and state committees.

Donna earned her B.S. degree at the University of Oregon and has completed graduate-level work at Lewis and Clark College, Portland State University, and the University of Oregon. As part of her work to create differentiated learning options for students in content areas, Donna designed a program entitled "Voices of Injustice," which the National Middle School Association recognized as one of four exemplary programs in the nation for 2001. Donna's own personal teaching style has always centered on providing differentiated instruction for the students in her classroom, and her personal goal is to validate and support the academic achievement of all students.

Donna can be reached at batesd10@yahoo.com.